VLADs

FOR

DUMMIES®

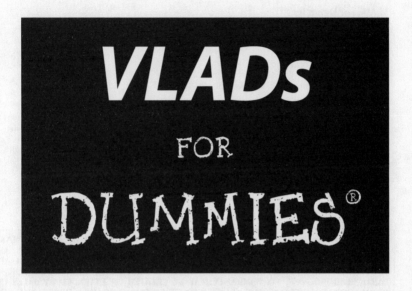

VLADs
FOR
DUMMIES®

by Clinical Practice
Improvement Centre

**Queensland
Government**
Queensland Health

WILEY

Wiley Publishing Australia Pty Ltd

VLADs For Dummies®

published 2008 by
Wiley Publishing Australia Pty Ltd
42 McDougall Street
Milton, Qld 4064
www.dummies.com

Copyright © 2008 Wiley Publishing Australia Pty Ltd

ISBN 978 0 7314 0829 0

Printed in Australia by
McPherson's Printing Group

10 9 8 7 6 5 4 3 2 1

Authors' Acknowledgements

The following people at Queensland Health's Clinical Practice Improvement Centre and external contributors were involved in the development of this book:

Authors

Stephen Duckett

Michael Coory

Maarten Kamp

Justin Collins

Kirstine Sketcher-Baker

Kew Walker

Technical Writer

Rosemary Moore

Special Thanks

Peter McNair

Josie DiDonato

Mark Mattiusi

Sue Cornes

Chris Hall

Publisher's Acknowledgements

We're proud of this book; please send us your comments through our Dummies online registration form located at www.dummies.com/register/.

Some of the people who helped bring this book to market include the following:

Acquisitions, Editorial and Media Development

Project Editor: Maryanne Phillips

Acquisitions Editor: Charlotte Duff

Editorial Manager:
Gabrielle Packman

Production

Layout and Graphics:
Wiley Composition Services,
Wiley Art Studio

Cartoons: Glenn Lumsden

Proofreader: Marguerite Thomas

Indexer: Karen Gillen

Contents at a Glance

Table of Contents

Introduction

*1*n 2005, a scandal surfaced concerning a surgeon employed in a Queensland public hospital. Investigations, set up to find out what exactly happened and how, concluded that Dr Jayant Patel, Director of Surgery at Bundaberg Hospital, was responsible for the deaths of eight patients at that hospital over two years, and may have contributed to the deaths of eight more.

The Bundaberg tragedy came on the heels of events elsewhere in Australia that seriously jeopardised patient care in Western Australia, the Australian Capital Territory and New South Wales. An editorial reflecting on these events noted:

Not surprisingly, all these incidents had common characteristics: Compromised patient safety not detected by sentinel event reporting; suboptimal clinical governance; health care professionals, who, frustrated by inaction after internal reporting of adverse events, brought the matter to the attention of politicians; and, finally, all incidents provoked one or more independent inquiries.

> Van der Weyden MB, 2005, 'The Bundaberg Hospital scandal: The need for reform in Queensland and beyond', Medical Journal of Australia, *vol. 183, pp. 284–5.*

The Bundaberg hospital tragedy became a rallying call to hospitals and health departments everywhere. For Queensland, home to the most recent events, hard questions had to be asked. What was it about reporting and monitoring at the time that so dramatically failed? How could such an event be avoided in the future?

Massive changes occurred in Queensland hospitals, the health department and the ministry. They resulted from reviews and reports that exposed problems with existing monitoring and governance. Recommendations in the 'Forster Review' and the 'Davies Commission report' saw changes to the Health Services Act and within Queensland Health. The Clinical Governance Framework was substantially reviewed and transformed. A Clinical Governance Policy now overarches policies relating to management, networks, complaints, audit, performance reporting, appraisal and development, credentialing and conduct. The organisation structure of Queensland Health was revised, with new units responsible for improving patient safety, changing the organisation culture and improving the performance orientation and transparency.

This brings us to the purpose of this book. The introduction of VLADs across the state is just one aspect of the changes. The VLAD (Variable Life Adjusted Display) system is a tool for spotlighting extraordinary trends and occurrences at or near the time they occur — so they can be investigated, pronto. Other clinical governance standards introduced or re-developed relate to roles and responsibilities, risk management and patient satisfaction.

The VLAD system incorporates all of the principles that have informed the changes to the health system:

- ✔ Line management responsibility for patient safety and quality
- ✔ Clinician and patient involvement
- ✔ A just and open approach to managing adverse events
- ✔ Responsibilities articulated for all levels of Queensland Health
- ✔ Measurement of outcomes and performance
- ✔ Transparency and accountability
- ✔ Emphasis on the need for Queensland Health to improve its performance in patient safety, quality and effectiveness

VLADs are being used to monitor outcomes of care in the 87 largest public and private hospitals in Queensland. These hospitals account for 83 per cent of all hospital activity in the state.

The changes have been wide-ranging and have called for new understandings, procedures and skills. This book is one means by which it is hoped that staff may find their way confidently through the new system.

About This Book

This book is meant to be used as a resource by anyone who has anything to do with VLADs. You may want to start by skimming or just dip in. Or you may want to read the whole thing and better understand why this tool has been introduced, and why it's a vastly improved way of ensuring public safety and confidence in the health system.

The VLAD system is formally called Variable Life Adjusted Display, but you may be on more intimate terms with VLADs by now, so we stick with this abbreviation throughout this book.

Like all 'For Dummies' books, *VLADs For Dummies* is written for intelligent people who simply want more information about an important topic. The book is designed to make the subject of VLADs more accessible to everyone, as well as providing pointers to where you may go for additional information.

How This Book Is Organised

The book is divided into four parts, roughly covering the what, how and where to go for more information on VLADs.

Part 1: Coming to Terms with VLADs

The VLAD process may seem confusing and be somewhat frustrating at first, so the chapters in this part are designed to explain what the new system is all about and what it's all for. It explains how VLADs get drawn, what flagging is all about, and the types of patterns that trigger flags and control levels. Confused? If you're coming to VLADs cold, Part I is a good place to start.

Part II: Getting on Top of Investigations and Reports

You need this information in this part if you're wondering what happens after a notification — the time when people are brought together, questions are asked, charts are checked and follow-up actions are thought through.

Part III: The Part of Tens

Whether it's the place where you finish reading or the place where you drop in, this part ties up some loose ends and anticipates your questions. You might want to refer to this part first if you think you know the VLAD basics and just want to check on one thing. Contacts, resources and common questions are all included.

Part IV: Appendixes

The appendixes at the end of this book provide additional VLADs reference material. Most are resources that are also available online, but we include them here so that everything is at your fingertips.

Icons Used in This Book

Throughout this book, icons flag information of special importance.

Some handy stuff is highlighted with this icon. If you're just skimming through, you'll find useful summary information that you won't want to forget.

Some tips will save you time; others will save you confusion and bewilderment.

We include a few explanations and definitions that we call 'technical', but some of it is simply complicated — interesting to some readers, but not essential for everyone.

 This icon flags resources available online.

Where to Go from Here?

Keep this book with you as you go through whatever VLAD-related task you encounter in your work. Time and experience should resolve any complications you first encounter. Keep asking questions, if you need to. Contact information is found in Chapter 8, covering the top VLADs resources.

Please provide feedback on this book to:

Clinical Practice Improvement Centre

Tel: 07 3636 9889

Email: vlad_queries@health.qld.gov.au

Part I
Coming to Terms with VLADs

Glenn Lumsden

*'No need for concern.
That's not your blood pressure,
that's our VLAD chart.'*

In this part . . .

You've become involved with VLADs — maybe you're part of an investigation triggered by a VLAD flag or maybe you're involved in building or interpreting VLADs.

Chapter 1 explains what VLADs are and why Queensland Health uses them. Chapter 2 explains the VLAD basics: How VLADs are put together and what data is used. It also covers all you want to know about clinical indicators and expected and actual outcomes. Chapter 3 introduces you to flagging, including an explanation of the upper and lower control limits, and the patterns that lead to flagging.

Chapter 1

VLADs: Why They Exist and What They're for

• •

In This Chapter

▶ Discovering what VLADs do

▶ Getting your head around the investigation process

▶ Seeking extra help

• •

*V*LAD. It's a weird name, right? But it identifies a very useful thing.

A VLAD (Variable Life Adjusted Display) is a type of statistical control chart or graph. Originally used in other workplaces to measure machine performance and learn when a machine needed to be recalibrated, repaired or removed, VLADs are now used in lots of different industries, including health. If you're working with VLADs, you might be plotting, calculating, analysing, flagging, notifying, being notified, investigating or reporting.

The introduction of VLADs — pronounced *vlads*, sort of like the Transylvanian guy — by Queensland Health was inspired by the need to better monitor treatment outcomes (for example, patient readmission to hospital). Of course, improving patient monitoring calls for more focused and strenuous follow-up of unexpected outcomes. So VLADs are a critical piece of a broader picture.

All about VLADs

Queensland Health's VLAD is a monitoring tool and a little bit more. The VLAD records patient outcomes in a precise way that also allows for unexpected trends to be seen. In addition, the outcomes for a clinical indicator in a particular hospital or facility can be plotted against state averages, and the points at which one hospital's or facility's outcomes go significantly above or below the state average are automatically marked as needing review and explanation. The VLAD also helps focus everyone's attention: Pointing to where to look to improve quality of care. So these little graphs are a highly effective visual way to identify where a possible problem or improvement may have been made, and mark these for follow up.

Outcomes from a procedure, such as hip replacement, do vary from hospital to hospital, and even from period to period within the same hospital. Variations are usually just coincidental, but sometimes they're the outcome of a real shift in practice or treatment quality. The VLAD is the starting point of a process that looks for patterns that might indicate either a problem or an inspired practice change that has actually improved outcomes.

VLADs are simply graphs, technically known as statistical process control charts. Each chart shows outcomes for a particular clinical indicator — 30 indicators are currently used. The data comes from routine data collections (which presently include the Queensland Hospital Admitted Patient Data Collection and the Perinatal Data Collection — although data sources may change in time). See Chapter 2 for more on clinical indicators and data sources.

The clinical indicator data is plotted for a particular period for a particular hospital (or a facility — but to keep things simple, this book refers to only hospitals from here onwards) and is available via Indicator Reports. If the graph reveals a different pattern in relation to average outcomes across the state, this pattern is visible on the VLAD. If it departs from the state average in a statistically significant way (or shows flags — using a system known as control limits), the hospital is notified via the Notification Report, so that an investigation of clinical cases forming part of the pattern can be instigated.

Who needs to know about VLADs?

The use of VLADs is governed by an implementation standard, included in Appendix A. Even though this book mainly refers to hospitals using VLADs, the standard applies to:

✔ Health Service Districts and other elements of Queensland Health that provide clinical services

✔ Area Health Services and Area Clinical Governance Units

✔ The Private Health Unit of Queensland Health

✔ Clinical Practice Improvement Centre

✔ Patient Safety and Quality Board

✔ Level 3 VLAD Responses Sub-committee

Notifications range from level 1 (a 30 per cent relative increase or decrease compared to the state average for mortality indicators) to level 3 (a 75 per cent relative increase or decrease compared to the state average for mortality indicators). For more information on flagging, notification levels and control limits, see Chapter 3.

Investigating and Reporting Following a Notification

A notification triggers an investigation in the hospital. The process goes something like this: The Indicator Reports and Notification Report are received, the investigation is conducted, actions arising from the investigation outcome are worked out and implemented, then all of this is reported and the report is reviewed (this process is described in more detail in Chapter 4).

Officers (VLAD reviewers) appointed by the district manager or chief executive in each hospital receive the monthly VLAD reports and then coordinate the investigation. The VLAD reviewers need to consult the appropriate people and work out the parameters of the investigation. To help with these parameters, Queensland Health offers the Pyramid Model of Investigation, which suggests approaching the investigation by beginning with the broadest category, the data (used to create the VLAD). The model then steps you progressively through other tiers. As you approach the pointy end, you get closer to the less likely causes. Aspects of the investigation, including the Pyramid Model, are discussed in Chapter 4.

The VLADs system is about improving patient safety, treatment and outcomes. You're invited to get to know the process, understand why it's needed, remember the experience of Bundaberg and aim to help make the VLAD system work, even if understanding it may seem burdensome. Remember too that ultimately, VLADs can significantly reduce your workload by filtering out areas where there's less likely to be a concern and providing a list of cases to review further.

Different types of actions will follow from your investigation. A hospital may develop a new policy or procedure or conduct a further review, for example, of current priorities related to equipment used. Or the hospital may wish to look into bed allocation practices. Chapter 5 offers some examples of actions that follow from various levels of the Pyramid Model.

The final stage for the hospital is to report the investigation and proposed actions or actions undertaken. The report format and content to cover is discussed in Chapter 6. This chapter also discusses tabling responsibilities and public reporting of outcomes.

Getting More Information

We cover all the basic VLAD information in Chapters 2–6. However, this book also includes supplementary information, including answers to common VLADs questions and helpful VLADs resources. You can find important policy and procedures documents in a series of appendixes at the end of this book.

Before moving on to another chapter, note that this book — and other measures like it — is intended to simplify the VLAD system by helping everyone involved to understand it a little better. Understanding the whole process is one way of making your role in it more meaningful and more effective.

Although the VLAD system is part of relatively new clinical improvements and governance, the system is being sharpened and refined even now. Feed your thoughts and any difficulties through to Queensland Health, and in this way help to streamline it and make it easier to use and understand for everyone involved. Email the Clinical Practice Improvement Centre on `vlad_queries@health.qld.gov.au`.

Chapter 2

A VLAD Is an Uncommonly Useful Graph

• •

In This Chapter

▶ Introducing the clinical indicators

▶ Applying clinical indicators to a VLAD

▶ Finding out where the data for VLADs comes from

▶ Understanding how a VLAD is created

▶ Checking out what the VLAD identifies

• •

*I*magine a hospital is consistently performing better than expected in a specific area — for example, in reducing complications from knee replacement or reducing mortality from pneumonia. What if this happens in one period of the year, but not in others? Is it because a particular doctor is rostered on at this time, or because an especially canny and experienced coder is working on the records? Or maybe an individual person had nothing to do with the great result: Maybe the credit goes to a new system or resource.

Such examples show a really important aspect of the VLAD system: The opportunity to identify a good outcome and then pinpoint what may have helped it to happen. Out of this arises the opportunity to make systematic changes that keep the good outcomes coming.

The VLAD system was adapted for health outcomes by Chris Sherlaw-Johnson. For a background on VLADs, see Sherlaw-Johnson's 2005 article 'A method for detecting runs of good and bad clinical outcomes on Variable Life-Adjusted Display (VLAD) charts' in *Health Care Management Science*, vol. 8, pp. 61–5.

In Queensland, VLADs are part of a relatively new process of monitoring clinical outcomes. A VLAD is a visual representation of trends in outcomes for certain clinical indicators — and VLADs can show trends in a quite precise way. Unexpected trends are flagged for investigation (see Chapter 3).

VLADs allow hospitals to see how they're performing on a number of measures. On the VLAD, the hospital can see how its actual outcomes on a given measure compared with the expected outcomes on that measure over a set period. If the chart shows a shortcoming on a given measure, the hospital needs to investigate. (You find out more about carrying out investigations in Chapters 4, 5 and 6.)

Although the events at Bundaberg that triggered the shake-up of the hospital system concerned an individual doctor, VLADs are about more than clinical practice. This book explains the Pyramid Model of Investigation for possible reasons in Chapter 4 — at this point, though, you simply need to know that investigations occur in five broad areas, which start with how good the documentation in the patient record is, and include things like the process of care as well as issues relating to individual professionals.

The best type of VLAD investigation uncovers why something happened the way it did and does something about it. For example, in the case of a positive outcome, the investigation prompts ideas for making further improvements or focusing research attention; in the case of a negative outcome, it generates ideas about changes to prevent such outcomes occurring again.

But first — this chapter takes a look at the measures used to indicate performance. Later in the chapter, you find out how a typical VLAD is created.

Clinical Performance Indicators

Queensland Health uses lots of different indicators to monitor how health services are performing. Some are quite new, introduced in the clinical governance initiatives talked about in the Introduction. But only certain indicators are being used in VLADs.

Introducing the VLAD clinical indicators

Table 2-1 shows the current clinical performance indicators being used for VLADs. The clinical performance indicators are grouped by disease, condition or procedure type according to four outcomes: Complications of surgery, readmission, long stay and mortality. A group called maternity is also listed, which looks at caesarean sections and inductions of labour.

Table 2-1	Current Clinical Performance Indicators by Outcome
Outcome	**Indicators**
Complications of surgery	Laparoscopic cholecystectomy
	Vaginal hysterectomy
	Abdominal hysterectomy
	Colorectal carcinoma
	Knee replacement
	Hip replacement
	Prostatectomy
	Fractured neck of femur
Readmission (public only) and long stay (public only)	Acute myocardial infarction
	Heart failure
	Knee replacement
	Hip replacement
	Depression
	Schizophrenia
	Paediatric tonsillectomy and adenoidectomy

(continued)

Table 2-1 *(continued)*	
Outcome	*Indicators*
Mortality	Acute myocardial infarction
	Heart failure
	Stroke
	Pneumonia
	Fractured neck of femur
Maternity	Selected primiparea caesarean section (public)
	Selected primiparea caesarean section (private)
	Selected primiparea induction of labour

To view indicators and their definitions, including the actual codes used, see Appendix B. These may change, so check www.health.qld.gov.au/quality/vlad.asp for the most up-to-date listing.

Thirty clinical indicators are currently being used in the VLAD system. More clinical performance indicators are planned for the future. These include venous thromboembolism readmissions, in-hospital falls, antibiotic prophylaxis administration and pressure ulcers. Still others may be added.

Why these indicators?

Why choose these indicators? Well, they didn't all just fall into line right at the start. A process of selection, review and refinement was undertaken — the tasks went to various committees, sub-committees and working groups.

To begin, a much larger set of potential measures was put up for grilling, including indicators from Australia, such as those used by the Australian Council of Healthcare Standards, and from overseas, especially from Ontario, Canada. However, a big set would have become unmanageable and would have become onerous for everyone involved. So some criteria were applied to trim the group. The criteria for selecting the list of indicators listed earlier in this chapter were:

- **Significance:** The clinical significance in terms of the burden of the disease
- **Volume:** Was there sufficient numbers of patients to provide a statistically reliable measure?
- **Indicator clarity:** It had to be clearly defined and reliable
- **Responsive potential:** The disease, condition or procedure type had to be able to be systematically improved (there's no point including a measure that can't be improved when the need for improvement has become clear)

The proposed indicators were reviewed by clinicians to check they measured something useful! For example, an orthopaedic network suggested hip and knee replacement readmission indicators, because this would assist in monitoring, if excessive numbers of patients were readmitted to other public Queensland hospitals as well as the treating hospital, with complications attributable to the initial surgery.

What was wrong with the old way of reporting?

The old way of reporting clinical indicators entailed basically the same indicators but these were only reported on once a year, with data reporting the current and previous two years hospital mean, compared against the peer hospital mean and the state mean. One of the problems was that the old method didn't encourage analysis of what was going on within a year: Runs of good and bad performance were obscured in a single annual figure. Another problem was that reports happened up to 16 months after any event that could have raised alarms. So if something was going seriously wrong or seriously well, this way of reporting data wasn't necessarily going to show it — and almost certainly wasn't going to show it at the time it was happening and needing attention.

Clinical expert groups generously gave their time and knowledge to help select the indicators. After the indicators were identified, each was (again) exhaustively reviewed and refined — and this process continues as Queensland Health refines them following more experience with monitoring and as clinical practices and coding change.

Your Average VLAD

What are the essential characteristics of a VLAD? Well, each VLAD investigates one clinical indicator:

- ✔ According to a particular outcome
- ✔ Against a particular cut-off for reactive increase or decrease
- ✔ For a particular period
- ✔ For a particular hospital
- ✔ By each patient

The x-axis is the sequence of cases plotted over time. Each point on the graph represents an individual patient. For mortality indicators, the y-axis is the estimated statistical lives gained, based on the probability calculation described later in this chapter (in 'Step 1: Calculating probabilities and risks'). Similarly, for complications indicators, the y-axis represents estimated statistical complications avoided; for readmission indicators, readmissions avoided. The long stay indicator measures the estimated number of patients who didn't stay an excessive length of time in the hospital (long stays avoided).

Take a look at the example shown in Figure 2-1. The major elements of a completed VLAD are displayed.

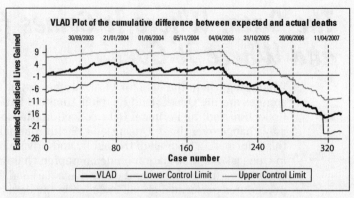

Figure 2-1: Acute myocardial infarction in-hospital mortality.

Source: Lamington State Hospital, 1 July 2003 to 31 July 2007.

In the VLAD shown in Figure 2-1, the clinical indicator is acute myocardial infarction. Each patient is represented on the VLAD line according to the outcome of interest: In-hospital mortality related to acute myocardial infarction.

✔ The period is 1 July 2003 to 31 July 2007.

✔ The hospital is Lamington State.

✔ Each patient treated for this clinical indicator in the given period is included on the VLAD.

✔ It also shows how Lamington State resulted in statistical lives lost at the end of the period graphed. These are described as *statistical lives* because you're looking at a statistical pattern and tracking probabilities of death. Over time, even if a hospital performs only slightly worse than the state average, this will add up and the VLAD will show more statistical lives lost. In the case of Lamington State, each small difference added up so that at the end of the graph 16 extra statistical lives had been lost over the period July 2003 to July 2007.

✔ Upper and lower control limits are also shown (for more information on these limits, turn to Chapter 3).

The Data: Where It Comes from and Where It Goes

Wondering where the data for VLADs comes from? Current sources are the Queensland Hospital Admitted Patient Data Collection and the Perinatal Data Collection (the sources may change over time). Queensland Health routinely collects this information from all of the public and private hospitals in Queensland. Information on demographic characteristics of patients, the principal and other diagnoses and the procedures performed are all included in the data collection.

The VLAD system requires a fast turnaround — hospitals need to provide their routine data within 35 days from the end of the month (phew!). It's a big ask, but it permits a much more timely and effective way of tracking and improving quality of patient care.

The Clinical Practice Improvement Centre in Queensland Health's corporate office analyses the data for the 30 clinical indicators and creates an individual Indicator Report for each VLAD graph. The VLAD Indicator Reports are provided to each hospital monthly, along with a Notification Report indicating which VLADs hospitals are to investigate (more on this in Chapters 3 and 4). Hospitals then analyse and investigate the VLADs and report on the outcomes of any reviews (as covered in Chapters 4 to 6). First, though, it helps to understand how a VLAD is put together.

Making a VLAD: Step by Step

A VLAD is created in a number of small but significant steps. The first is to calculate certain probabilities around each clinical indicator. Then each case (which really means each patient) is plotted on the VLAD.

Step 1: Calculating probabilities and risks

The first step is to calculate the probability of a particular outcome for a given indicator. This probability is used when plotting individual cases on the VLAD.

The probability is calculated, based on information available at the time of admission, that a particular patient (described in terms of their age, sex and co-morbidities as recorded in the data sets used) has a particular outcome. This probability is a number between zero and one and is also called the *expected risk* or the *expected outcome*. In the Queensland system, four main outcomes apply:

- ✔ Death
- ✔ Complication
- ✔ Readmission
- ✔ Long stay

The expected probability is the risk (in that person) of an adverse outcome, as measured at the time of admission, assuming their risk is the same as the average risk across all hospitals for all patients admitted for the same procedure or condition and with the same age, sex and co-morbidity profile as the patient in question.

This probability is calculated using logistic regression, with the adverse outcome the dependent variable, and age, sex and co-morbidities the independent variables.

Adding in age, sex and co-morbidity (a process known as *risk adjusting*) helps to ensure that hospitals or clinicians who see sicker patients are not unfairly viewed or even penalised. These co-morbidities were chosen based on criteria including their frequency of occurrence within the various cohorts (based on diagnosis codes other than the principal diagnosis), specialist medical advice, evidence from literature (where it existed) and statistical significance about how much the co-morbidity affected the outcome.

Check www.health.qld.gov.au/quality/vlad.asp for the most up-to-date listing of co-morbidities.

The probabilities are calculated using 12 months of data: The index month (or the month in question) plus the previous 11 months. The data includes results from patients as defined by each indicator admitted to public and private Queensland hospitals with at least an average of 20 patients a year for the relevant indicator.

After the risk adjusted probabilities are done, the VLAD compares the expected outcome as predicted by the risk adjustment equation with the actual outcome — and that's the basis for the VLAD.

A VLAD is a plot of the cumulative difference between expected and actual outcomes over a period of time. That is, in each case, between the probability of an adverse outcome and what actually happened: 1 or 0, depending on whether the adverse outcome happened or not.

Step 2: Plotting the first patient

The first case to be plotted is the first patient in the period who meets the clinical indicator criteria. In Figure 2-2, the indicator is in-hospital mortality related to acute myocardial infarction. The VLAD increases or decreases depending on whether the patient recovers or dies. How much it increases or decreases by depends on the probability of the patient with this condition dying, adjusted for age, sex and selected co-morbidities.

In this example, the probability of this patient dying is 0.3. The patient has recovered, so the VLAD increases by 0.3. The VLAD shows the increase by plotting 0.3 on the *y*-axis at the point of case number 1.

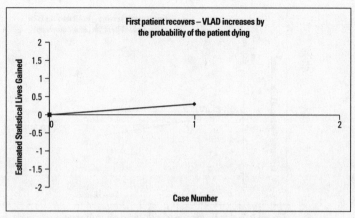

Figure 2-2: Acute myocardial infarction in-hospital mortality. In this example, the first patient recovers.

But what if the first case to be plotted is a patient who didn't recover? Figure 2-3 shows the alternative scenario — same indicator, different outcome. In this example, the probability of the patient dying is still 0.3, therefore the probability of the patient surviving is 0.7. The patient has died, however, so the VLAD decreases by 0.7. The VLAD shows the decrease by plotting −0.7 on the *y*-axis at the point of case number 1.

A positive outcome (recovered, no complications) is attributed a 0, with the adverse outcome a 1. The actual movement in the VLAD graph is calculated as the difference between the expected outcome and the actual outcome. If the calculated risk of death is, say, 0.3, and the patient died, then the graph descends to −0.7 which is obtained by calculating 0.3 − 1.

Another way of describing this is to say that a VLAD graph of mortality ascends when the patient recovers and descends when the patient dies (or has complications).

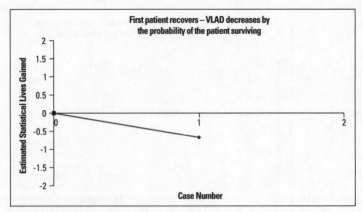

Figure 2-3: Acute myocardial infarction in-hospital mortality. In this example, the first patient dies.

In the case of mortality indicators, the graph increases or decreases according to the alternative outcome figure: If the patient dies, it's the probability of survival figure that's used; if the patient recovers, it's the probability of death figure that's used.

How much the graph increases or decreases depends on the probability that a patient recovers or dies when looking at mortality indicators. If a patient is older with numerous co-morbidities, they will have a higher probability of death than, say, a younger patient with no co-morbidities. Therefore, if the older patient with numerous co-morbidities dies, the graph would decrease by a lesser amount when compared to the younger patient with less co-morbidities. This example is used as the basis for the next step.

Step 3: Plotting the second patient

The second case to be plotted, shown in Figure 2-4, is the second patient in the period who meets the clinical indicator criteria.

Remember, for a mortality indicator, the VLAD increases or decreases depending on whether the patient recovers or dies.

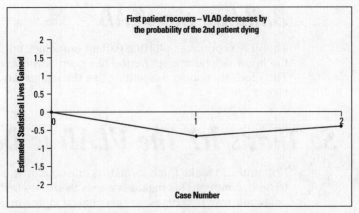

Figure 2-4: Acute myocardial infarction in-hospital mortality. In this example the second patient recovers.

In this example, the probability of the patient plotted second dying is 0.3. The second patient has recovered, so the VLAD increases by 0.3 from –0.7. The VLAD graph shows the increase by plotting –0.4 (–0.7 + 0.3) on the y-axis at the point of case number 2.

But what if the second patient dies? Figure 2-5 shows a VLAD on which is plotted two deaths when the probability of surviving is 0.7 for each patient. As you can see, the line now descends to –1.4.

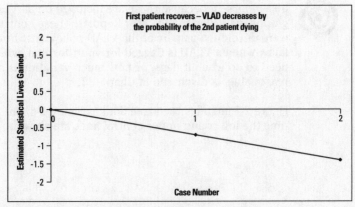

Figure 2-5: Acute myocardial infarction in-hospital mortality. In this example the second patient dies.

Building the VLAD

The VLAD continues plotting patient outcomes until all of the information for a set period has been accounted for. The VLAD then looks something like the image shown in Figure 2-6.

So That's It? The VLAD is Done?

Not quite. To make the information meaningful, it needs to be in context. This means it needs to show whether the hospital's own outcomes for this clinical indicator are within a range of reasonable variation mostly due to chance.

The whole point of the VLAD is to identify whether there are major differences between your hospital and others. That's what the control limits are for.

The VLAD shown in Figure 2-7 shows the line representing the cumulative difference between expected and actual outcomes enclosed by lines representing upper and lower *control limit lines*. The upper and lower lines are the control lines. If the hospital's cumulative difference line touches one of these control lines, that touch-point is flagged, indicating your hospital is different to the rest of the state.

No need to fear, you don't need to calculate the control lines yourself, because these are included on all VLAD graphs displayed in Indicator Reports. These control lines were developed as part of the VLAD policy. Just how you know when a VLAD is flagged for your hospital, what you need to do when it flags, or how much variation is seen as reasonable, is discussed in Chapter 3.

Figure 2-7 includes the same data as Figure 2-6, but this time the lower and upper control lines are shown.

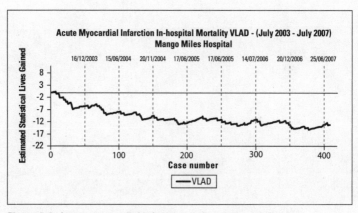

Figure 2-6: Acute myocardial infarction in-hospital mortality.

Source: Mango Miles Hospital, July 2003 to July 2007.

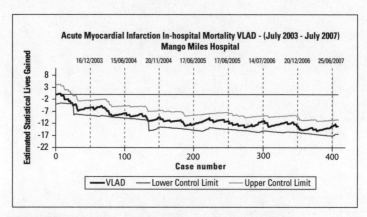

Figure 2-7: Acute myocardial infarction in-hospital mortality.

Source: Mango Miles Hospital, July 2003 to July 2007.

VLADs demonstrate high points and also alert you to potential problems. They have the potential to reveal processes and practices that improve patient safety and patient care. So watch the ascending lines as well as the descending lines — some VLADs are going to reveal great opportunities for exploring ways to improve patient care and safety.

Before acting on a flag marked on a VLAD, check out Chapter 3. To investigate and report on a flag, see Chapters 4, 5 and 6.

Chapter 3

A Flag on a VLAD Calls for a Closer Look

*Y*ou know those ball games and the excitement when a ball reaches the boundary? Whistles are blown, brows are furrowed and one team looks a bit sheepish or curses the umpire. Or, in some games, a ball going beyond a boundary causes a great cheer to rise up from the stands and admiring questions to be asked about the team that got it so far.

In the case of a VLAD, a boundary is fashioned according to the average reached in a particular health outcome by hospitals throughout the state. Kicking the ball within this area isn't going to raise either eyebrows or cheers: It's likely to be part of a normal pattern. But for VLADs, the outer boundaries, representing 30, 50, 75 and 100 per cent beyond that average boundary, are the trigger points for flags.

This chapter tells you what it means when you receive a VLAD that's flagged and how you will be notified. Only flagged VLADs require action, and different flags signify different levels of action.

Introducing Flags

When a flag appears on a VLAD it means: 'This warrants a closer look'. It doesn't mean that care in your hospital is bad; it might mean that you haven't recorded everything correctly in the patient record. So a flag is run up to say 'Look at me!'

Here's the reasoning behind the process. When a VLAD is created for a particular indicator, outcome, hospital and period, some sort of assessment needs to be made to see how that particular hospital's outcome compares with those of other hospitals. Only in this way can a judgment be made about whether the outcome is within the average range, or whether it's gone beyond the norm and therefore calls for an investigation to explain the extraordinary result. So a set of flagging criteria has been worked out that balances the effort and costs of investigating false signals (where variation occurs due to chance) against the need to identify true variation in outcomes.

A flagged VLAD should not be taken to mean good or bad performance. Lots of factors can cause a flag, including chance. The flagging capacity of the VLAD highlights issues for further review.

Take a look at the flagged VLAD shown in Figure 3-1. The two pointy arrows show where the flagging occurs.

False outcomes versus true variations: Balancing the cost

The flagging criteria is used to find an acceptable point between costly investigations of false signals — due to chance — and necessary investigations of true variations in outcomes. It's similar to the trade-off between sensitivity and specificity for a screening test. (Sensitivity is the proportion of true positives correctly identified by a screening test and specificity is the proportion of true negatives.) The VLAD model aims to minimise false flags but be sensitive enough to detect true flags in a timely manner.

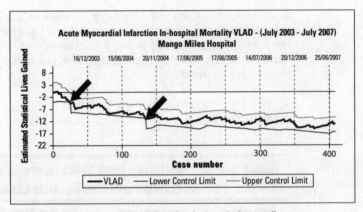

Figure 3-1: Acute myocardial infarction in-hospital mortality.

Source: Mango Miles Hospital, July 2003 to July 2007.

When a flag occurs, the whole process starts afresh and the control limits are reset. Statistical process control started in industry — if something was going wrong in a production line, you'd stop the line, fiddle with the machine (reset it), and start the process again. Same with VLADs. VLADs flag when something happens, then the control limits are reset and what happens from then is tracked. Is the system back 'in control' or is the same underlying trend continuing? Has any action taken by the hospital fixed the problem or not?

Notification Levels and Control Limits

Other than looking at every Indicator Report for all clinical indicators monitored at your hospital each month, there's an easier way to know if a VLAD has flagged. A monthly Notification Report is disseminated to your hospital and this includes a list of flagged clinical indicators (if any) and their notification levels.

If you receive notification of a flagged indicator, it's labelled with one of three notification levels. A level 1 notification is the lowest level. The higher the level, the more the outcome varies from the state average. Remember, the variation can be positive or negative.

Table 3-1 shows the percentage variation that triggers a notification flag.

Table 3-1	Variation from State Average and Equivalent Notification Levels	
Extent of Variation from State Average	*For Mortality Indicators*	*For Non-Mortality Indicators (Complications, Readmission and Long Stay)*
30 per cent	Notification level 1	N/A
50 per cent	Notification level 2	Notification level 1
75 per cent	Notification level 3	Notification level 2
100 per cent	N/A	Notification level 3

The notification levels obviously increase by degree of variation from the state average. Although these are most important in identifying instances of possibly compromised quality of care, it's worth reiterating that positive outcomes exceeding the state average are also worth investigating. The intention is for VLAD flagging criteria to equally serve to highlight practices that improve the quality of care, and to be measures that everyone can learn from.

Moving up the flagging or notification levels means that there are larger and larger variations from the state average. It also means that the variation is less likely to be caused by chance — and that means higher variations move to higher organisational levels to be looked into.

Within an Indicator Report, there are three VLAD graphs displaying the level 1, level 2 or level 3 upper and lower control limits. Figure 3-2 shows an example of a VLAD displaying the level 2 control limits.

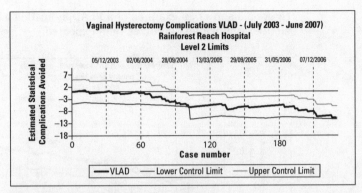

Figure 3-2: Vaginal hysterectomy complications.

Source: Rainforest Reach Hospital, July 2003 to June 2007

You discover more about the actions and reports required for each notification level in Chapters 4, 5 and 6.

You may be wondering how the upper and lower control limits are worked out. For more information on this, see Appendix A.

Patterns That Lead to Flagging

VLADs don't confirm that an error has occurred or that an outstanding result has been achieved. VLADs show trends. They hint at how a system is performing. They reveal trends that merit inspection and discussion. In this way, VLADs point to possible advances or problems and the need for investigation.

Have a look again at Figure 3-1, earlier in this chapter, showing two flagged points. Notice that each flag marks a patient during a downward trend in patient outcomes. The flag indicates that up until this patient there were more deaths than expected, resulting in a cumulative experience of poorer outcomes. Although Figure 3-1 shows a run of poor outcomes, it could just as well be a run of good outcomes. This cumulative experience is incredibly important. It could point to repeated errors that could become endemic and therefore need to be stopped and examined. It could point to procedures or treatments that may be improving quality of care and therefore need to be looked into, perhaps as areas requiring further research and spreading good news.

Figure 3-3 shows an example of a VLAD indicating a greater number of positive outcomes than expected.

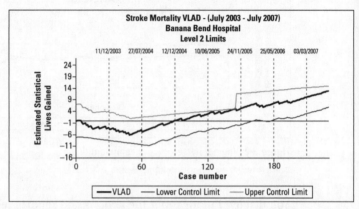

Figure 3-3: Stroke mortality. Banana Bend Hospital, July 2003 to July 2007.

Flagging means the investigator has to look back in time prior to the flag to determine why the flag has occurred. Figure 3-4 gives all the information from Figure 3-2, except it highlights a particular 'run' of cases that stimulated the need for an investigation. (More on investigations is covered in Chapters 4, 5 and 6.)

Figure 3-4 demonstrates one of four basic patterns. VLADs are visual and VLAD patterns appear in four basic configurations, which are shown in Figure 3-5. The different patterns lead to different start points for investigations.

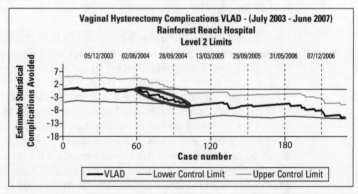

Figure 3-4: Vaginal hysterectomy complications. Rainforest Reach Hospital, July 2003 to June 2007.

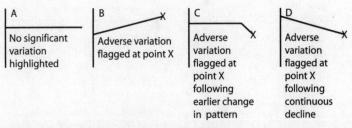

Figure 3-5: Typical patterns of outcome variation.

In Figure 3-5, Pattern A shows no significant variation. Pattern B shows a positive upward variation, which is flagged at point X. Figure 3-4 is an example of Pattern C, a negative downward variation flagged at point X following a change in pattern. Pattern D is a negative downward variation of continuous decline, flagged at point X. Figure 3-1 shows this sort of pattern.

The patterns help identify the periods that need investigation. In the case of Pattern C, the investigation particularly checks what occurred at the time that the curve changes and thereafter. Investigations into Pattern D focus on systematic underlying trends throughout the period of decline.

VLADs are visual. Step back and look to see if you can spot a clear pattern or problem period before you get buried in the detail. The control limits help you assess the play of chance. If the VLAD line crosses a control limit, then chance is an unlikely explanation and it's useful to investigate other possible explanations.

Chapter 4 describes a model to follow when conducting an investigation. It offers a continuation of the discussion of the VLAD chart to help you to pinpoint the periods and cases that need to be investigated.

Part II
Getting on Top of Investigations and Reports

Glenn Lumsden

In this part . . .

1f you're doing an investigation triggered by a flagged VLAD, or if you're wondering about an investigation result, this part is for you.

Chapter 4 looks at what happens when an investigation is to proceed: Who's involved, what's involved and how to use the Pyramid Model for the investigation. Chapter 5 is about action — the types of actions that follow an investigation. And in Chapter 6 you can read about how the investigation gets reported.

Chapter 4

Moving Forward with an Investigation

• •

In This Chapter

▶ Receiving the notification

▶ Understanding what happens after a notification

▶ Identifying key staff to involve in an investigation

▶ Investigating according to the Pyramid Model

• •

The preceding chapters explain the VLADs basics, including what they're for, how they're created and how notification levels work. This chapter now gets down to the hands-on tasks for hospitals: Investigating the reasons for a VLAD trend that deviates from the state average, or highlights a period in which the trend differs from the previous periods. These instances are flagged on VLADs and presented in the Indicator Reports, and if they go beyond the control limits this is indicated in a hospital's Notification Report with the notification set at level 1, 2 or 3.

A notification means an investigation needs to be done. The type of investigation depends on the level of the notification (see 'Acting on the Notification Level' later in this chapter). Figure 4-1 maps out the actions that follow a VLAD notification.

Hospital/facility receives monthly
VLAD Notification Report

Hospital/facility conducts investigation
of flagged VLADs

Hospital/facility submits VLAD Response Report,
including proposed or completed actions, to the
Clinical Practice Improvement Centre via the online
feedback form or email feedback form

VLAD Response Reports are reviewed by the
Clinical Practice Improvement Centre, Area
Clinical Governance Unit or the Private Health
Unit to ensure that if a problem exists, appropriate
actions are implemented

Figure 4-1: The key steps that follow a VLAD notification.

Who Receives the Notification?

Hospitals receive VLAD Indicator Reports and VLAD
Notification Reports monthly from the Clinical Practice
Improvement Centre (formerly Quality Measurement and
Strategy Unit) in Queensland Health. These are sent to the
VLAD reviewers nominated by the relevant district manager
or chief executive.

District managers or clinical executive officers nominate
the VLAD reviewers in each facility. Each district manager
or clinical executive officer also keeps a register of the
nominated VLAD reviewers for each facility, as well as a
record of the indicators these reviewers have access to.

Area general managers and the chief health officer must also keep an up-to-date register of appropriate reviewers in their units and the indicators the reviewers have access to.

Staff eligible for nomination as lead clinicians or reviewers are

- ✓ Hospital executive
- ✓ Clinicians
- ✓ Managers
- ✓ Quality improvements officers
- ✓ Decision support officers
- ✓ Health information managers
- ✓ Others as deemed appropriate

VLAD reviewers are given access to Indicator Reports. The Indicator Reports are currently disseminated as individual hospital and indicator-specific Excel workbooks containing a description of the VLAD methodology, the definition of the indicator monitored by the VLAD graph, the data behind the graph, and some handy tips on what questions to ask when investigating the VLADs. The Indicator Reports are available on a secure Web site, which VLAD reviewers also use to submit Response Reports on the outcomes of investigations. These reports may also or alternatively be sent through a password-protected CD.

Nominated reviewers are notified electronically by Notification Reports when their Indicator Reports are available on the secure Web site. For reviewers accessing Indicator Reports via CD, Notification Reports are included on the password-protected CD.

Notification Reports provide a summary of indicators within a hospital, Health Service District or an Area Unit that are newly flagged or previously flagged but an investigation has not yet been submitted or is incomplete.

For more information on who needs to be involved in an investigation following a notification, read on.

The VLAD Implementation Standard in Appendix A includes a list showing all the roles and responsibilities — who does what — in relation to VLADs dissemination and reporting.

Acting on the Notification Level

As you can see in Table 4-1, a level 1 notification requires an internal investigation and then a report to the relevant Area Clinical Governance Unit in Queensland Health (or the Private Health Unit) via the online feedback form or email feedback form. But a lower level 3 notification requires an investigation involving the hospital and relevant unit (such as the Area Clinical Governance Unit) in Queensland Health, as well as a report to the Level 3 VLAD Responses Sub-committee and Patient Safety and Quality Board. So the first thing to observe is the level of notification.

If multiple flags are triggered for the same indicator in the same reporting period, a report is only required on the highest level flag.

Table 4-1	Actions and Reports by Notification Level	
Notification Level (Mortality and Non-mortality)	Investigation Required	Type of Report
1	Internal investigation	VLAD Response Report sent via the online feedback form or email feedback form
		VLAD Response Report required within 30 days of notification

Notification Level (Mortality and Non-mortality)	Investigation Required	Type of Report
2	Internal investigation with Area Clinical Governance Unit or Private Health Unit involvement	VLAD Response Report sent via the online feedback form or email feedback form

VLAD Response Report required within 30 days of notification

Area Clinical Governance Unit (public) or Private Health Unit review VLAD Response Report |
| 3 | Internal investigation with Area Clinical Governance Unit or Private Health Unit involvement | VLAD Response Report sent via the online feedback form or email feedback form

VLAD Response Report required within 30 days of notification

Area Clinical Governance Unit (public) or Private Health Unit review VLAD Response Report

VLAD Response Report of all lower level 3 flags is reported to Level 3 VLAD Responses Sub-committee and Patient Safety and Quality Board subsequent to 90 days since initial notification |

A flag is just that, a flag to look more closely. It doesn't mean that the hospital has better or worse outcomes than overall. What is a sign of good quality is that the hospital responds to the flag in a timely way and undertakes an appropriate investigation to see what's really happening.

Identifying Other Related Indicators

In assessing a flagged VLAD, ask yourself, is there another clinical indicator monitored that relates to the indicator under investigation that may assist in identifying the cause of the notification? For instance, after receiving a notification for Heart Failure Mortality, a review of other cardiac VLADs for similar trends that occur at similar times within a hospital can assist in determining the cause of the notification. Likewise, readmission and long stay indicators for a condition should be reviewed in conjunction, because a higher number of readmissions can indicate that patients may not have had a long enough stay in hospital.

What to Cover in an Investigation

An investigation following a notification needs to include a few essentials. The investigation must-do's are

- ✔ Identify which periods and cases to investigate (discussed in this chapter)
- ✔ Identify and consult with key staff (discussed in this chapter)
- ✔ Investigate — this must include auditing the codes and documentation (discussed in this chapter; note especially the Pyramid Model of Investigation)

| ✔ Report results (For more information on reporting the investigation see Chapter 6; note that reports need to encompass the actions to take outlined in Chapter 5.)

Determining Which Periods and Cases to Investigate

A flag is placed at the point where the VLAD line meets the upper or lower control point. It marks a case; say, case 61. It suggests that during a window of time, more or less patients than average experienced the outcome. Overall, the hospital experience is so much better (for upper flags) or worse (for lower flags) than average that chance is an unlikely explanation for the better or worse result.

Is there a change in the trend? This is the first matter to resolve. A consistent decline or incline is a *no trend change*, whereas a decline or incline inconsistent with a previous pattern is a *trend change*. Either case warrants investigation, if the VLAD line meets an upper or lower control limit.

Always look at the overall pattern. (Remember the discussion about patterns in Chapter 3 and shown in Figure 3.5?) This helps you see what's changed or whether there's a continuous pattern.

The case that hits the control limit is not the only one that should be looked at. You also need to take into account all the preceding cases that lead to the flag.

No change in trend

The example in Figure 4-2 shows two flags highlighting a no trend change. In both cases you can see a *consistent* decline (representing adverse outcomes) among the patients before the case that has been flagged.

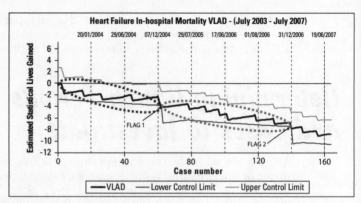

Figure 4-2: Consistent decline, no change in trend. Flags are preceded by consistent declines.

Here's two ways to go about the investigation:

✔ For lower level flags, investigate all patients experiencing the outcome from the last flag (if a flag has occurred before) to the flag point. Investigating an upper level flag is similar; however, patients *not* experiencing the outcome are investigated. If a flag has not occurred prior to the flag under investigation, patients from the beginning of the graph should be included in the investigation.

✔ An alternative way of investigating is to identify all patients since either the beginning of the graph or the last flag and focus on differences between cases with and without the outcome.

Table 4-2 summarises the options for investigating a no trend change.

Table 4-2	Investigating a No Trend Change	
Options	**If a Previous Flag is on the VLAD**	**If No Previous Flag is on the VLAD**
Option 1: For lower level flags, look at all patients experiencing the outcome. For upper level flags, include patients not experiencing the outcome	Investigate between the previous and current flag point. Results of the previous investigation(s) should be considered in the current investigation.	Investigate from the beginning of the VLAD graph to the current flag point
Option 2: Identify all patients in the period and focus on differences between cases with and without the outcome	Investigate between the previous and current flag point. Results of the previous investigation(s) should be considered in the current investigation.	Investigate from the beginning of the VLAD graph to the current flag point

Change in trend

Take a look at Figure 4-3 — it shows two distinct periods of rapid declines. Either a sudden increase or sudden decline indicates a change in trend (the trend change). Sudden or distinct changes give you additional clues about what you should investigate: When did this particular 'run' of cases that led to the change begin? What may have caused the change in the pattern?

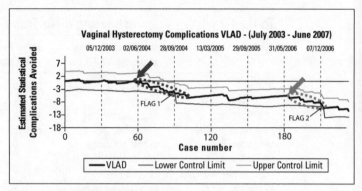

Figure 4-3: Distinct changes in trend.

So, in these situations, the investigation needs to look at

✔ Whether there were changes in hospital staffing or patient management practices around the time the trend changed (approximately around the time case number 60 and case number 183 were discharged in Figure 4-3)

✔ Identify the patients with the outcome from the change in trend until the lower limit is crossed (patients without the outcome would also be investigated, if an upper limit is crossed). An alternative approach is to identify all patients between the change in trend and the case where the lower control limit is crossed. The focus in this approach should be on differences between cases with and without the outcome.

Consulting with Key Staff

Received a notification? The first thing you need to do after assessing the Indicator Report and identifying which periods and cases to investigate, is to identify all the individuals, units and divisions within the hospital or facility that need to be involved. Notify them as quickly as possible that an investigation is underway and that their cooperation is needed. The turnaround for lower levels notification is tight, so action needs to happen quickly.

Table 4-3 shows the key staff who need to be involved. References in this table to the Pyramid Model, covered later in this chapter, provide guidelines for conducting consultations.

Table 4-3	Key Staff Involved in Consultations
Who	*Role in Investigation*
Clinical coders Health Information managers Clinical benchmarkers Risk managers	At least one of these staff to be consulted for each level of the Pyramid Model (discussed later in this chapter). They can contribute to checking documentation and case mix issues, as well as helping with summarising the data.
Unit director Nurse unit manager Other clinicians	At least one of these staff to be consulted for each level of the Pyramid Model (covered later in this chapter)
District manager or executive officer	Reviews investigations results and the management action plan of each investigation
Area Clinical Governance Unit or Private Health Unit	Involvement in reviews of levels 2 and 3 flags (refer to 'Acting on the Notification Level in this chapter)
Level 3 VLAD Responses Sub-committee and Patient Safety and Quality Board	Involved in reviews of lower third level flags (refer to Queensland Health Clinical Governance Implementation Standard – Variable Life Adjusted Display, Appendix A)

The Pyramid Model of Investigation, discussed next in this chapter, highlights that you begin your investigation by involving staff with experience in looking at data: The health information managers and coders. Queensland Health recommends that doctors and other clinicians are also involved, because the coding relies on clear and correct documentation of patient conditions and treatments. Many adverse events are caused by communication issues, so involve team members from different disciplines. So at all stages, many members of the care team are involved.

Following the Pyramid Model of Investigation

You can investigate a notification in many different ways. A considered and sensible approach suggested by Queensland Health is to use the Pyramid Model of Investigation, outlined in this section. Individual institutions may want to investigate their own way — it's up to institutions to decide. But the approach using the Pyramid Model is designed to thoroughly cover most possible reasons to explain why a flag has occurred.

 The Pyramid Model, formally called the *Pyramid Model of Investigating Hospital Performance* was first proposed by Mohammed MA, Rathbone A, Myers P, Patel D, Onions H, and Stevens A, in 2004, in 'An investigation into general practitioners associated with high patient mortality flagged up through the Shipman inquiry: Retrospective analysis of routine data' (*British Medical Journal*, vol. 328, pp. 1474–7).

Reasons for a notification occurring are many and varied. The Pyramid Model, shown in Figure 4-4, recognises multiple explanations and recommends that the most likely explanations are checked first.

Figure 4-4: The Pyramid Model of Investigation.

Notice the range of possible reasons for a notification. The broadest category, data, at the base, is the point at which to start your investigation. It's the most likely of all the five possible causes of a notification. As you approach the pointy end, you get closer to the less likely causes.

The Pyramid Model of Investigation is a hierarchical model in the sense that the more likely reasons are clustered at the broad base and the less likely reasons are found at the pointy apex.

A note to clinical coders: Having data at the base and pinpointing data error as the most likely cause *does not* suggest that people involved in record entry are more likely to commit error than other health workers involved in activities at the apex of the pyramid. Instead, it recognises that many individuals, factors and time-related issues are involved in the coding process — sometimes the coder can be at the end of a chain of error and innocently enters the data as it has been provided by others. Working with data can be a messy business (which is why it's the broadest category in this pyramid), and it's understood that many coders spend a lot of their working time just trying to straighten things out. Further, coders can only code what's in the record. If the documentation isn't clear or inclusive from the start, there'll be problems at every point in the chain.

Pyramid level 1: Data

In the early stages of any look at data, you'll nearly always find problems, so first up, look at the quality of the data. Check whether there's a conflict between charts and codes, and charts and discharge summary documentation. Errors occur when clinicians provide chart notes that are unclear, incomplete or just plain wrong. Sometimes clinicians fail to provide any record of key diagnoses that might affect whether the outcome was likely. Coders, too, sometimes err, neglecting to record an additional diagnosis that's affected the outcome, or misclassifying the principal diagnosis. Follow up any data issue that could have caused the outcome: Interrogate data accuracy, chart reliability, definitions and completeness.

Data questions to ask

- ✔ Has the data been coded accurately?

- ✔ In each case you look at, has the principal diagnosis been assigned correctly? The *principal diagnosis* is defined as the diagnosis established after study to be chiefly responsible for occasioning an episode of admitted patient care.

- ✔ Have all possible additional diagnoses been coded (this may affect the risk adjustment)? Was a potential additional diagnosis, indicated through a pathology report, not recognised and treated in this episode?

- ✔ Have the conditions present on admission been coded correctly?

- ✔ Has there been a change in data coding practices?

- ✔ Is all clinical documentation clear, complete and consistent?

- ✔ Have the definitions been used correctly?

- ✔ Is the data complete?

Pyramid level 2: Patient case mix

The next step is to investigate patient case mix. Is there a case mix variation that has not been fully taken into account in the risk adjustment process (see Chapter 2) and that would contribute significantly to the patient group investigated being different from the rest of the state? An example might be all patients who experienced complications of surgery but who were excessively obese, which contributed significantly to the complications experienced.

Consider all variations that may be excluded from the risk adjustment. For example, Indigenous status is often linked to worse clinical outcomes — for example in heart clinical performance indicators. However, Indigenous status is not included in the risk adjustment model. Indigenous status alone *should not* be accepted as a reason for poor clinical outcome — Queensland Health wants to improve quality of care for everyone!

Patient case mix questions to ask

✔ Are there factors particularly affecting patients at this hospital that haven't been taken into account in the risk adjustment?

✔ Has the pattern of referrals to this hospital changed in a way not taken into account in risk adjustment?

✔ Have patients been admitted for palliative care or were 'Not for Resuscitation' orders in place? (These obviously affect outcomes but aren't coded in the routine data set, so they're not used in risk adjustment.)

✔ Was a potential additional diagnosis, indicated in a pathology report, not recognised and treated in this episode?

Pyramid level 3: Structure or resource

If the patient case mix questions don't turn up any results, check whether, in the period under investigation, structural or resource issues could have influenced the outcome. Hospitals' structures and resources change frequently and patient outcomes can be affected by availability of beds, staff and medical equipment. Institutional processes might also have had an impact — so too, could resources outside the hospital. An example is an unexpectedly long stay at a mental health facility because of a shortage of beds or services in the community.

Structure or resource questions to ask

✔ Was there a change in the distribution of patients in the hospital: For example, were more patients in this specialty spread throughout the hospital rather than concentrated in a particular unit?

✔ Was length of stay affected by availability of community services?

✔ Could any other structure or resource changes influence the outcome in some way?

Pyramid level 4: Process of care

The next step is to look at process of care. This includes changes in hospital or treatment approaches. A possible suspect is changes to treatment practices — for example, the introduction of a new clinical treatment guideline could affect clinical outcomes in a positive way. Another example is the effect of a key staff member being away on leave, such as the education worker who explains after-hospital care to parents of kids who've had their tonsils out.

If there hasn't been a distinct change in the pattern of the VLAD graph, you need to look at how things are done in the hospital. Is there an agreed guideline, care path or protocol for this condition in the hospital, at the state level or promulgated by a professional society? If so, has it been consistently followed in the treatment of all cases (or all cases within an adverse outcome)? You may find the case control analysis approach (see Appendix A) helpful in trying to identify process of care issues.

 Look further afield! If the facility you're investigating hasn't published process of care guidelines, you may find it useful to visit another, similar hospital with good outcomes and explore its typical care paths or protocols.

Process of care questions to ask

- ✔ Was there a change in the care path followed?
- ✔ Could the outcome be due to changes in patient admission and discharge policies at the hospital?
- ✔ Have new treatment guidelines been introduced?
- ✔ Does the care in this hospital follow normally accepted guidelines?

Pyramid level 5: Professional

The final step in the Pyramid Model is to look at the clinical staff. Maybe changes in staff occurred during the period under investigation. Or the staff may have stayed the same, but their skills or methods changed because of recent training. Lots of things can affect patient outcomes: Changes in practice and practitioners, and treatment methods. An example is a higher number of biliary leaks due to the inexperience of a laparoscopic surgeon.

Professional questions to ask

- ✔ Was there a change in staffing for treatment of patients?
- ✔ Has a key staff member gained additional training and introduced a new method that has led to improved outcomes?
- ✔ Are the cases with adverse outcomes all or mostly associated with one clinician or one team?

All the pyramid levels discussed in this section outline the nuts and bolts of an investigation. The next chapter takes these elements of the Pyramid Model and considers the sorts of actions that may arise from findings in each of the five levels.

The investigation is the most critical part of the whole VLAD process. The graphs are simply designed to highlight when an investigation needs to occur and make it easy to identify which cases to investigate.

Chapter 5

Acting on an Investigation

• •

In This Chapter

▶ Looking at actions that address particular findings

▶ Understanding that actions are integral to the investigation process

• •

*A*n investigation might turn up one, or a number of findings. However many there are, after identifying the reasons for the outcomes, the hospital needs to act — or work out what actions it will take — before reporting on the investigation.

A key part of the investigation is the actions introduced to correct an adverse outcome (or in the case of a positive outcome, entrench it, mark it as a subject for research, or tell others about it). Some examples of possible findings and the sorts of actions that might be taken to address these findings are included in this chapter. More information on reporting is covered in Chapter 6.

Examples of Actions Based on the Pyramid Model

The Pyramid Model of Investigation, described in Chapter 4, is comprised of five areas that could affect outcomes — data, patient case mix, structure or resources, process of care, and professional. Although hospitals are free to decide on their own actions, this chapter includes some examples of how outcomes caused by the different pyramid factors might be dealt with. It's useful to think about a process such as this when working out your hospital's approach.

Tables 5-1 to 5-6 run through actions that could conceivably follow particular findings. Hopefully, you'll find them helpful when working out what actions to explore or implement based on the findings to your investigations.

Table 5-1	Examples of Actions Following a Data Investigation
Findings	*Actions*
A coding error: For example, a missed additional diagnosis or wrong principal diagnosis classification	Correct coding and resubmit data to ensure flag no longer occurs Educate coders Conduct regular coding audits Provide incentives to improve coding accuracy
Unclear, incomplete or inaccurate chart notes from clinicians	Correct coding and resubmit data Educate clinicians Encourage closer liaison between coders and clinicians to verify any queries relating to documentation Promote use of VLAD Coding Query Flowchart to coders or HIMs (see resources in Chapter 8)
Conflicting documentation between charts and discharge summary documentation	Correct coding and resubmit data Educate clinicians Educate coders Encourage closer liaison between coders and clinicians to verify any queries relating to documentation Conduct regular documentation audits Provide incentives to improve documentation accuracy
Conflicting documentation between codes assigned and charts	Correct coding and resubmit data

Table 5-2	Examples of Actions Following a Patient Case Mix Investigation
Findings	*Actions*
An unaccounted-for case mix variable, for example, patients with the adverse outcome were 'Not for Resuscitation' or were receiving palliative treatment	Review each patient for appropriateness for hospital admission given their 'Not for Resuscitation' status or where receiving palliative treatment Audit admission or SNAP codes for palliative care-type patients and see whether the admission coding was appropriate
An unaccounted-for case mix variable, for example, a high percentage of Indigenous patients were among the people experiencing the outcome	Review each patient to see if the most appropriate treatment was provided Consider developing community-based programs to effect change in outcomes for Indigenous patients Encourage staff participation in the Cultural Awareness Program and other training programs to ensure delivery of culturally appropriate health care Consider if the delivery of services is culturally appropriate. Assistance from Indigenous Health Liaison Officer could be sought to determine this

Table 5-3	Examples of Actions Following a Structure or Resource Investigation
Findings	*Actions*
A lack or absence of resources (for example, beds, staff, community services)	Develop policies and procedures to manage treatment of patients outside the agreed Clinical Services Capability Framework where the hospital doesn't have this capacity Include issue as part of budget and service planning exercises being undertaken at Health Service District, Area Health Service and Queensland Health level

(continued)

Table 5-3 *(continued)*

Findings	Actions
Different equipment or technology availability	Review priority setting for related equipment
Patient mix affecting outcomes (for example, surgical patients in medical wards)	Find out if this is an unusual occurrence or a regular pattern Examine whether bed allocation reflects the clinical needs in the facility

Table 5-4   **Examples of Actions Following a Process of Care Investigation**

Findings	Actions
Less than 100 per cent compliance with clinical pathways, standardised protocols, standardised guidelines and so on	Measure or monitor variance from clinical pathways, standardised protocols, published guidelines and so on Determine whether variance relates to an individual practitioner and, if so, action as per professional findings (see Table 5-5) Determine whether variance relates to more than one practitioner and, if so, consider education sessions or systems that make compliance with the guideline automatic

Table 5-5   **Examples of Actions Following a Professional Investigation**

Professional Findings	Actions
Staff fatigue	Ensure staff are relieved as required by guidelines: Has the hospital got a fatigue risk management plan? Is it being followed?
Use of a different clinical technique producing worse outcomes	Introduce clinical pathway Encourage doctors' adherence to a clinical pathway

Professional Findings	Actions
Poor or questionable clinical practice or a doctor operating outside of credentials or appropriate score of practice	Refer to the Clinician Performance and Remediation Standard (for doctors); the Queensland Nursing Council Scope of Practice Framework for Nurses and Midwives; or, for other staff, the local performance management guidelines

Digging a Little Deeper

Actions are integral to the investigation process. Here are some extra points to keep in mind when you're investigating flags and considering appropriate actions.

✔ **Data investigation:** When data quality issues are found to be a reason for a flag, rectify the coded data set as soon as you can. Make all alterations in your submitted data so it can be taken into account in the next month's VLAD. Resubmitted coding changes will be reflected in subsequent VLADs. When coding has been identified as an issue and the data corrected, updated VLADs may not show flags in future.

If future VLADs still show flags and no other data-related reason for the flag has been identified, then look more closely at other levels of the Pyramid Model (outlined in Chapter 4).

✔ **Patient case mix investigation:** Although risk adjustment removes variation due to case mix variables, not all can be adjusted this way. Some variables can't be included in the risk adjustment because they occur infrequently, whereas some aren't included because they simply aren't coded. Refer to the Indicator Definition section of your VLAD to find out what variables have been adjusted. More information about risk adjustment is included in Chapter 2.

A policy decision has been taken to not adjust for Aboriginal or Torres Strait Islander identification as part of risk adjustment, even though, on average, Indigenous patients have worse outcomes. If you identify that flagging has been driven by adverse outcomes in

Indigenous patients, don't stop there! You need to think about what you need to do differently for Indigenous patients, their families and communities to improve their outcomes. Perhaps think about further cultural awareness training of hospital staff or changes that can be made to the way health care is delivered to Aboriginal and Torres Strait Islanders.

✔ **Structure or resource investigation:** Resource needs may be internal or external to hospitals, so your investigation may need to consider both possibilities.

✔ **Process of care investigation:** Are the processes of care at your hospital the most up to date? Why not check out other hospitals or facilities that have an upper level flag to see what they do?

When you've checked out the tables in this chapter and figured out the most suitable actions to take in light of your investigation findings, you need to devise a timeline for completing the actions. Timelines for implementation are part of the investigation report, covered in Chapter 6.

Having trouble working out what would be an appropriate action? Advice is available from your Area Clinical Governance Unit.

Chapter 6

Reporting the Investigation

• •

• •

*A*fter receiving a notification and acting on it, guided perhaps by the Pyramid Model of Investigation covered in Chapter 4, the next step in the investigation is producing your VLAD Response Report.

The Response Report needs to describe what was investigated and what action has been taken or is planned.

The reporting format is developing and will be continually reviewed. But the essential elements of reporting are explained in this chapter.

What Form to Use for the Report

The hospital investigation probably involved a number of people asking a number of questions, and possibly some false starts. A brief report outlining the outcome(s) that lead to the investigation and the results and proposed actions from the investigation will be welcomed by everyone involved at the hospital concerned.

The report needs to provide a clear guide for action.

 Queensland Health offers a template reporting form, which is online at www.health.qld.gov.au/quality/vlad.asp. It includes everything your report needs to address.

The next section runs through the parts of the template that need to be completed by the hospital.

What to Report

The form requests some minimal detail about the subject of the feedback: The nature of the VLAD and the outcomes being followed up (for example, fewer or more deaths than expected). It asks for information about which cases were investigated and which units were consulted in the investigation.

You need to include a description of the number of charts where a problem is identified and the nature of the problem.

Investigation description, outcomes and actions

The report needs to detail the reviews that were conducted (for example, coding audits and clinical review), and what the reviews found. Include a description of the number of charts where a problem is identified and the nature of the problem. The report also needs to describe how hospital management has acted as a result of the review or what actions still need to be put in place. Record all types of actions and the date when each action was or is expected to be completed.

If you used the Pyramid Model to investigate flags, you'll report on findings from each pyramid area (data, case mix, structure or resource, process of care, and professional). Perhaps you used a different approach, but any approach is likely to include coding audits and other elements of that pyramid.

For each area defined on the Pyramid Model (data, case mix, structure and so on), describe

- ✔ **What was done:** The type of investigation conducted
- ✔ **What was found:** The results of the investigation

As well, describe these four elements of the management action plan

- ✔ What the hospital plans to do based on the investigation results (policy and practice change)
- ✔ The steps that will be taken to ensure better compliance with the changed policy or practice
- ✔ How and where the changes will be monitored within the hospital or at other levels (for example, by district) so that progress can be tracked
- ✔ When the changes or actions will commence or are expected to be complete

Report endorsement

Before the report is submitted, the district manager or executive officer is expected to review and endorse it, ensuring a thorough investigation has occurred. The report provides the person submitting the VLAD Response Report the opportunity to indicate if this has occurred.

Assessing the Report

Depending on the level of the flag, the hospital feedback form is assessed by the

- ✔ Area Clinical Governance Unit
- ✔ The Private Health Unit
- ✔ Clinical Practice Improvement Centre
- ✔ Patient Safety and Quality Board (for reports investigating lower level 3 flags)

A level 3 flag is considered to be statistically significantly different from average state performance, so the report of the investigation is scrutinised at the highest level.

Your Response Report is assessed by all levels on correct interpretation of the VLAD, extensiveness and independence of the review, and if the management action plan addresses identified issues.

How Results Are Considered and Publicly Reported

Your VLAD Response Report needs to say whether and how the investigation report will be considered by your hospital, such as by the peak Health Service District committee responsible for quality and safety and at the Health Community Council for Queensland Health facilities, and whether it's considered locally or corporately for private hospitals.

Summary VLAD reports for each hospital will be included in the Annual Public Hospital Performance Report. This public report highlights level 3 flags and includes information about any reviews that came about as a result of flagging, including management action plans.

The report is not the end of the process. What needs to happen is action to address any problems identified or to ensure good outcomes are maintained.

Level 3 reports are very important and are reviewed carefully at the most senior levels of Queensland Health. Don't forget that the level 3 flags indicate big differences from the state average. This means there needs to be serious and detailed review to identify why the flag occurred. A flag may not be the result of a serious clinical issue that affects patient care, but it might be. You need to look openly and honestly at why the flag occurred. And then you need to act on the results. If a data issue caused the flag, fix the data system. If a clinical issue was responsible, start the process of making sure the care in your hospital is up to state standard.

Part III
The Part of Tens

Glenn Lumsden

'She's such a great surgeon that
every time she walks into the hospital
our VLAD chart jumps up two points.'

In this part . . .

This part gives you useful information in handy parts (of ten). Here you can find ten answers to commonly asked questions about VLADs and ten important and practical resources.

Chapter 7

Ten Answers to Frequently Asked VLAD Questions

*I*f you're new to VLADs, you may well have dozens of questions! This chapter raises a few of the most frequently asked questions about working with VLADs, and provides some responses.

If you have additional questions, ask. Other employees in your hospital who have experience in VLADs are a great source of information. Please see also the resources listed in Chapter 8.

Why Does Queensland Health Use VLADs?

The Bundaberg Hospital scandal highlighted the need for accountability and reporting across all hospitals in Queensland. The VLAD methodology meets this need, offering Queensland Health a comprehensive way to monitor processes and the quality of services provided. The ability to track performance against key quality indicators, flag possible issues, and investigate and report on the investigation outcomes makes the VLAD system an important tool for transparency and quality.

How Do I Know When I Need to Investigate a Flag?

The Clinical Practice Improvement Centre sends you a notification, letting you know that a flag on a VLAD needs investigating. (For more information on Notification Reports, refer to Chapter 4.)

How Do I Know which Patients to Investigate?

First, look at the overall patterns on the VLAD. Can you see a change in the pattern on the graph? If so, determine at which point the graph changed and hover your mouse over that point. When was it? Did something change in the hospital around then? What was different? If the flag meets the lower control limit (a lower flag), investigate those patients experiencing the outcome, from the patient where the change in the pattern occurs to the point at which the graph is flagged. Follow a similar process for flags that meet the upper control limit (upper flags), except in these cases you only need to investigate the patients not experiencing the outcome.

If no change in pattern is obvious on the VLAD, identify all the patients between the last flag or the start of the graph until you reach the notified flag. Then, as per graphs that do show patterns, investigate patients experiencing the same outcome for lower flags, or all patients (even those not experiencing the outcome) for upper flags. To understand why you need to investigate upper flags, see the next section in this chapter. For more information on determining which patients are investigated, refer to Chapter 4.

Why Do I Need to Investigate Upper Flags?

Investigations into upper flags (flags triggered by the upper control limit) are conducted for two reasons.

Firstly, flagging can be due to coding errors or omissions — for example, the exclusion of co-morbidities or complications. Improving the coding is a good thing and, as well as helping to ensure the flagging is correct, it's also important for funding because of requirements in the Casemix Funding Model. That's why it's important that all data issues are rectified.

Secondly, when a flag relates to a process of care issue that improves patient outcomes, investigation and reporting of information can be shared among clinical networks so that hospital services can be improved statewide.

Why Are Three Different Flags Used?

The three different levels of flags (levels 1, 2 and 3) relate to the extent of variation between the hospital and state means. The higher the level number, the surer everyone can be that the variation is less likely to be due to chance. Higher level flag numbers need a greater level of accountability, creating the need for greater levels of governance.

How Do I Conduct an Investigation?

After you identify which patient cases need to be investigated, it's time to implement the Pyramid Model of Investigation. By working through the stages from the bottom of the pyramid up, you're able to identify or eliminate issues. Make sure you investigate each of the five tiers in the pyramid, even if you pinpoint the issue in one of the lower tiers. That way you can ensure that your investigation is thorough and complete.

When writing the report, it's important to note what you've done to investigate the flag even if an issue isn't clarified. For example

- ✔ Have you investigated the flag using every tier in the Pyramid Model of Investigation?
- ✔ What action are you taking in response to your findings — that is, what is your management action plan?

If your investigation doesn't pick up anything, talk to your Area Clinical Governance Unit or Private Health Unit.

What Do I Do after an Investigation?

Most importantly, you act on the findings! In terms of reporting, though, you send your investigation report to the Clinical Practice Improvement Centre using the current response process (refer to Chapter 6).

As part of your investigation report you will have identified some areas that need a management action plan (MAP). It's important to make sure that the actions are completed. MAPs are a good way of helping to prevent the same flag occurring in the next reporting month.

The Clinical Practice Improvement Centre may need some more information from you if it's not clear what was investigated or what MAP was put in place.

Are VLADs Statistically Valid?

VLAD methodology is adopted for Queensland Health and follows Sherlaw-Johnson's methodology based on statistical process control, mentioned in Chapter 2. The original statistical control methodology was developed several decades ago to improve the quality of manufactured products and is today used across several industries, including health. For resources on statistically in-depth information, check out Chapter 8.

Why Do I Have to Report to Queensland Health Centrally?

Queensland Health has a commitment to the public to deliver transparency and report on the quality of its health services. VLADs are not only contributing to fulfilling this commitment but are also used for benchmarking and in monitoring and identifying quality practice improvement. Level 3 flags occur only if a big variation is recorded. This may indicate that something is seriously wrong and is reportable to the Patient Safety and Quality Board. These flags also highlight any patterns emerging (indicating problems or solutions) across the whole state.

Where Does the Data Used in VLADs Come from?

All the data used to create the VLADs comes from information that hospitals currently submit centrally. This information is then obtained from Queensland Hospitals Admitted Patient Data Collection (QHAPDC), and the Perinatal Data Collection. That's why it's important to ensure that all the information you submit is accurate and complete.

Chapter 8

Ten Great VLAD Resources

*T*his chapter provides a list of some of the most important and useful resources that are available for people using VLADs. Most are journal articles available online — these can help to deepen your understanding of how VLADs work. Also listed are some key documents or tools that you'll need to refer to on your VLADs journey.

Want to know more? Remember that you can also phone (07) 3636 9889 or email vlad_queries@health.qld.gov.au if you want to ask more questions.

VLADs Methodology

Article: 'A method for detecting runs of good and bad clinical outcomes on VLAD charts'

Description: This key article from Chris Sherlaw-Johnson discusses the VLAD and CUSUM techniques for continuous monitoring.

Source: Sherlaw-Johnson C, 2005. 'A method for detecting runs of good and bad clinical outcomes on variable life-adjusted display (VLAD) charts', *Health Care Management Science*, vol. 8, pp. 61–5.

Monitoring Variations with VLADs

Article: 'Identifying variations in quality of care in Queensland hospitals'

Description: This recently published article describes the use of VLADs to monitor outcomes of care in the 87 largest public and private hospitals in Queensland.

Source: Duckett SJ, Coory, M, and Sketcher-Baker, K, 2007, 'Identifying variations in quality of care in Queensland hospitals', *Medical Journal of Australia*, vol. 187, pp. 571–5.

www.mja.com.au/public/issues/187_10_191107/
duc10459_fm.html

The Role of Routine Data as a Screening Tool

Article: 'Assessing quality using routine data'

Description: This article looks at the use of routine data to evaluate the quality of health care, concluding that current routine data is probably most useful as a screening tool that highlights areas in which quality should be investigated in greater depth, and that the growing availability of electronic clinical information will change the nature of routine data in the future, enhancing opportunities for quality measurement.

Source: Iezzoni L, 1997, 'Assessing quality using administrative data', *Annals Internal Medicine*, vol. 127, pp. 666–74.

www.annals.org/cgi/content/full/127/8_Part_2/666

How VLADs and Data Work Together

Article: 'Using control charts to monitor quality of hospital care with administrative data'

Description: This paper compares cross-sectional analyses with sequential monitoring using control charts, concluding that control charts provide an understandable and up-to-date overview that allows early detection of runs of good or bad outcomes that can help hospitals identify areas for more in-depth self-monitoring and learning.

Source: Coory M, Duckett S, Sketcher-Baker K, 'Using control charts to monitor quality of hospital care with administrative data', *International Journal for Quality in Health Care* 2007:1–9.

The Role of Control Charts

Article: 'The use of control charts in health-care and public-health surveillance'

Description: A valuable contribution to the discussion around using control charts

Source: Woodall W, 2006, 'The use of control charts in health-care and public-health surveillance', *Journal of Quality Technology,* vol. 38, pp. 89–104.

VLAD Coding Flowchart

Tool: VLAD Coding Query Flowchart

Description: This detailed flowchart shows you how to proceed if a coding question arises.

Source: Clinical Quality and Analysis Unit.

www.health.qld.gov.au/quality/vlad.asp and select VLAD Coding Query Flow Chart.

An Investigation into Patient Care

Tool: Interim Reporting Results Flowchart

Description: This flowchart describes requirements for reporting after a notification of a flag has occurred and explains what happens if a response is not received, is inadequate or accepted.

Source: www.health.qld.gov.au/quality/vlad.asp and select Interim VLAD Reporting Results Flowchart.

Accounting for Performance

Report: Queensland Public Hospital Performance Report 2006–07

Description: Chapter 7 in this report, covering safety and quality, provides an example of VLADs used in a public reporting scenario.

www.health.qld.gov.au/performance/docs/phpr_chapter_7.pdf.

Implementation Standard

Tool: Implementation Standard 4, Variable Life Adjusted Display, Dissemination and Reporting

Description: This standard describes the mandatory auditable requirements regarding the dissemination of the VLAD to Health Service Districts, Area Health Services, Private Health Unit and the Patient Safety and Quality Board.

 Source: See Appendix A or go to www.health.qld.gov. au/quality/vlad.asp and select 'VLAD Implementation Standard'.

Definitions

Tool: Variable Life Adjusted Display Clinical Indicator Definitions

Description: This extensive document tells you all you need to know about clinical indicators.

 Source: See Appendix B or go to www.health.qld.gov.au/ quality/vlad.asp and select 'VLAD Definitions'.

Part IV
Appendixes

Glenn Lumsden

'I put them there to remind me that
all this paperwork is worth it.'

In this part . . .

This part presents the book's appendixes. You only need to dip into these resources if you require backup information on VLADs.

Appendix A

Further Reading

● ●

*T*his appendix brings together some of the key documents associated with VLADs.

The first document, Figure A-1, outlines Queensland Health's policy on clinical governance. Figure A-2 details the VLAD Implementation Standard, and Figure A-3 explains how control limits are applied.

QHEPS Document Identifier: 32542

Queensland Government
Queensland **Health**

QUEENSLAND HEALTH
CLINICAL GOVERNANCE POLICY
Policy for all components of Queensland Health

Clinical Governance Policy

Effective:	01 July 2007
Review:	This document will be reviewed annually
Last Reviewed:	
Supersedes:	New Policy

POLICY

Safeguarding and improving the safety and quality of patient care is the first priority of Queensland Health and will inform all aspects of the work and decisions of constituent units.

Framework

The Queensland Health Clinical Governance framework are the policies, processes and accountabilities that are directed at improving patient safety and the quality, effectiveness and dependability of Queensland Health services. It does not replace, but is additional to, the professional self-regulation and individual accountability for clinical judgement that are an integral part of health care

Implementation

The following Implementation Standards specify the requirements that must be met to support the intent of the policy and framework:

1. Roles and Responsibilities

2. Clinical Risk Management Plans

3. Patient Satisfaction Survey

4. Variable Life Adjusted Display (VLAD)

Fundamental elements of Queensland Health's approach to clinical governance

1. Line management responsibility and accountability for patient safety and quality;

2. All clinicians are responsible and accountable for patient safety and quality;

3. Safety and quality processes must involve patients;

4. A just and open approach for managing adverse events;

5. Responsibilities and accountabilities articulated at all levels of Queensland Health;

6. Measurement of outcomes and performance;

7. Transparency and accountability;

8. An emphasis on the need for Queensland Health to improve its performance in patient safety, quality and effectiveness of its' service delivery.

© The State of Queensland (Queensland Health) 2007
Page 1 of 3
Date: 19 April 2007

Figure A-1: Queensland Health's Clinical Governance Policy, page 1 of 3.

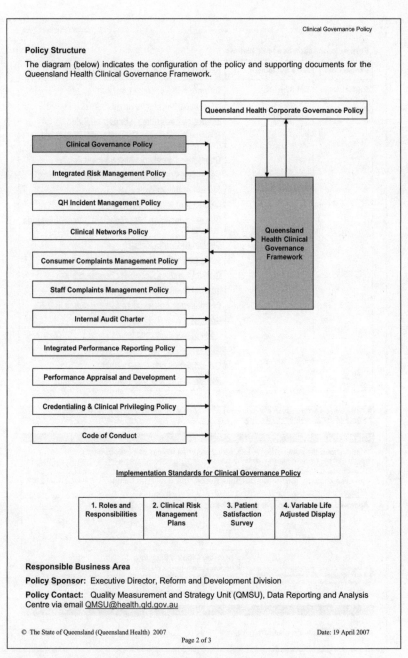

Figure A-1: Queensland Health's Clinical Governance Policy, page 2 of 3.

Further Information See links (below)

Procedures	Data Systems	Related Documents and Information Sites
Performance Appraisal for all clinical staff.	QH Risk PRIME CI PRIME CF	Corporate Governance Policy Integrated Risk Management Policy **Integrated Performance Reporting Policy** Queensland Health Credentialing and Scope of Practice Standard **Consumer Complaints Management Policy** **Consumer Complaints Implementation Standard** Staff Complaints Policy **QH Incident Management Policy** **Clinical Incident Management Implementation Standard** **Clinical Networks Policy** **Open Disclosure Project** **Clinical Services Capability Framework** **Internal Audit Charter** **Performance Appraisal and Development IRM 8.2** **Coroner's Act** **Code of Conduct 2006** Glossary of Terms – Quality Management Patient Safety and Quality Board **Health Quality and Complaints Commission**

Policies and relevant Implementation Standards are to be used in conjunction with Procedures, Work Instructions, Forms and Related Documents.

Release Details

Table A shows the administrative details for the current release of this document:

TABLE A	
Review authored by:	Senior Director, Data Reporting and Analysis Centre. Date: 19 April 2007
Approved by:	Executive Director, Reform and Development Division.

_____

Approving Officer's Signature

Figure A-1: Queensland Health's Clinical Governance Policy, page 3 of 3.

QHEPS Document Identifier: 32547

Queensland Government
Queensland **Health**

QUEENSLAND HEALTH
CLINICAL GOVERNANCE
IMPLEMENTATION STANDARD
4. Variable Life Adjusted Display – Dissemination and Reporting v3.4

Implementation Standard for all Queensland Health employees and agents – including Queensland Health Corporate Office, Statewide Services, Shared Service Providers, Area Health Services and Health Service Districts

1. Purpose:

Variable Life Adjusted Displays (VLADs) is a monitoring tool to be used for improving the quality of services provided. This standard describes the mandatory auditable requirements regarding the dissemination of the Variable Life Adjust Display (VLAD) to Health Service Districts, Area Health Services, Private Health Unit, the Patient Safety and Quality Board and its subcommittees. This standard uses terms and concepts defined in the <u>Queensland Health Clinical Governance Policy</u> and Glossary of Terms – Quality Management.

2. Scope:

This standard applies to:

- Health Service Districts and other elements of Queensland Health which provide clinical services and their staff;
- Area Health Services and Area Clinical Governance Units;
- Private Health Unit;
- Private hospitals;
- Mater Public Hospitals;
- Clinical Practice Improvement Centre;
- Patient Safety and Quality Board and its subcommittees.

3. Authorising Policy:

<u>Queensland Health Clinical Governance Policy</u>

4. Review:

This standard will be reviewed annually and revised if there are policy and process changes for:

- Corporate and clinical governance in Queensland Health
- Queensland Health information system for corporate and clinical governance,

This standard was last reviewed: December 2007. Current review: April 2008

Version: 3.4   Date: April 2008

Figure A-2: The VLAD Implementation Standard, page 1 of 8

5. Supersedes:

VLAD Implementation Standard v2.0

6. Business Contact:

Any requests for further information or clarification regarding this standard should be referred to the Clinical Practice Improvement Centre, Reform and Development Division Phone: 3636 9889.

7. Further information: see links below

Implementation Standards	Procedures	Related Documents
		Corporate Governance Policy
Roles and Responsibilities	Data Systems	Credentials and Clinical Privileges Policy
		Clinical Networks Policy
Performance Monitoring	QHAPDC	Clinical Incident Management Policy
Information System		Integrated Performance Reporting Policy
		Integrated Risk Management Policy
		Service Capability Framework
		Patient Safety and Quality Board
		Health Quality and Complaints Commission
		Glossary of Terms
		Health Services Act 1991

8. Variable Life Adjusted Display – Definition and Background

Variable Life Adjusted Display (VLAD) is a screening tool to identify the place to start in examining possible areas of concern (or strength) for safety and quality of care. It does this by "flagging" certain indicators which warrant further investigation. It should be interpreted and reviewed with the intention to understand causation and to determine whether corrective action is necessary. It is not a diagnostic tool. The VLAD significantly reduces workload by filtering out areas where it is less likely to be a concern and provides a list of cases to review further.

It is expected that Level 2 and 3 flags will stimulate a more rigorous investigation than Level 1 flags. This is because a Level 3 flag is less likely to be due to chance or random variation than a Level 1 flag. A flag is initiated where the VLAD line meets the lower or upper control limits. When a VLAD flags at a particular point it is suggesting that over time there have been more patients experiencing the outcome than expected, up until this patient. The suggested way of viewing this graph is to firstly look for flags and then look backwards from this flagging point to see if there is a change in the trend or not. It is what leads up to the point at which the VLAD line meets the control limit (*the track*) which is most important rather than the actual point itself (*the crossing*).

Figure A-2: The VLAD Implementation Standard, page 2 of 8

<table>
<tr><td colspan="2">Clinical Governance, Variable Life Adjusted Display Dissemination and Reporting</td></tr>
</table>

9. Variable Life Adjusted Display – Indicators

Variable Life Adjusted Display (VLAD) Indicators for 2008

Indicator ID Code	Indicator Name
C001-1	AMI In-hospital Mortality Rate
C001-3	AMI Readmission Rate
C002-1	Heart Failure In-hospital Mortality Rate
C002-3	Heart Failure Readmission Rate
C003-1	Stroke In-hospital Mortality Rate
C004-1	Pneumonia In-hospital Mortality Rate
C051-1	Fractured Neck of Femur In-hospital Mortality Rate
C051-2	Fractured Neck of Femur Complications of Surgery (Whole Admission) Rate
C052-2	Laparoscopic Cholecystectomy Complications of Surgery Rate
C053-2	Colorectal Carcinoma Complications of Surgery (Whole Admission) Rate
C054-2	Hip Replacement (Primary) Complications of Surgery (Whole Admission) Rate
C054-3	Hip Replacement (Primary) Readmissions within 60 days Rate
C055-2	Knee Replacement (Primary) Complications of Surgery (Whole Admission) Rate
C055-3	Knee Replacement (Primary) Readmissions within 60 days Rate
C055-4	Knee Replacement Long Stay
C056-2	Prostatectomy Complications of Surgery Rate
C057-3	Paediatric Tonsillectomy and Adenoidectomy Readmission Rate
C057-4	Paediatric Tonsillectomy and Adenoidectomy Long Stay
C101-5	Selected Primiparae Induction of Labour
C101-8	Selected primiparae Caesarean Section (Public Hospitals)
C101-9	Selected primiparae Caesarean Section (Private Hospitals)
C103-2	Abdominal Hysterectomy Complications of Surgery Rate
C104-2	Vaginal Hysterectomy Complications of Surgery Rate
C151-3	Depression Readmission Rate
C151-4	Depression Long Stay
C152-3	Schizophrenia Readmission Rate
C152-4	Schizophrenia Long Stay

10. Reporting protocols

A review of the VLAD is required where notification has been received concerning a flagged indicator. The **District Manager** or nominated accountable officer is required to complete a report within 30 days of notification which includes details of the indicator, the investigation undertaken and the management action plan to correct an unfavourable result or to maintain a positive result. These reports are to be submitted through the District Manager. Private facilities are required to report through their CEO. There is no current requirement for private facilities to report on upper level flags.

Figure A-2: The VLAD Implementation Standard, page 3 of 8

		Clinical Governance, Variable Life Adjusted Display Dissemination and Reporting	
Flags	**Fatal Outcome Indicator***	**Non-Fatal Outcome Indicator***	**Action Required**
1	30	50	Hospital will investigate internally and report outcome to Area Clinical Governance Unit or Private Health Unit (for Private Facilities), who will review the investigation.
2	50	75	Hospital will investigate internally and report outcome to Area Clinical Governance Unit or Private Health Unit (for Private Facilities), who will review the investigation.
3	75	100	Hospital will investigate internally and report outcome to Area Clinical Governance Unit or Private Health Unit (for Private Facilities), who will review the investigation. **Lower Level 3 flags:** Patient Safety and Quality Board will review hospital investigation and management action plans.

Reporting Rules:

- Area Clinical Governance Units are responsible for reporting on level three flags to the Patient Safety and Quality Board (PSQB). A level three flag is considered as being statistically significantly different from State average.

- In the case of multiple flags being triggered for the same indicator in the same reporting period, only the highest level flag needs to be reviewed and reported, as this review should include findings for the lower level flags.

The VLADs will be updated on a monthly basis using administrative data submitted through the Queensland Health Admitted Patient Data Collection and the Perinatal Data Collection. Any delay in submission of data from hospitals will influence the currency of the VLAD data dissemination.

Access to the VLAD information will be granted to officers nominated by members of the Executive Management Team. District Managers are to nominate officers within their Districts only.

Public Hospitals:

During the year, the regular updates to the VLADs will be disseminated via a secure web site so that appropriate review can be undertaken before any public disclosure occurs. Notification reports will be emailed to the relevant nominated officers. The results of the review process will also be captured online through a secure site. Any report submitted in this manner will require the endorsement of the District Manager.

Figure A-2: The VLAD Implementation Standard, page 4 of 8

Clinical Governance, Variable Life Adjusted Display Dissemination and Reporting

Private Hospitals:

VLAD data and notification reports will initially be disseminated by password-protected CD to private hospitals. The results of the review process will be returned by email utilising the forms provided on the CD.

In 2008, a secure online site will be available for the private hospitals to access and report on their VLADs in a similar manner to the process currently undertaken by public hospitals.

11. Roles and Responsibilities

The following roles and responsibilities apply with respect to this implementation standard.

Title /Role	Responsibilities
Corporate Level	
11.1 **Clinical Practice and Improvement Centre (CPIC)**	11.1.1 Analyse and disseminate indicators monthly
	11.1.2 Notify relevant parties of flagged indicators
	11.1.3 Manage feedback system for lead clinicians/reviewers and Area Clinical Governance Units/Private Health Unit
	11.1.4 Review hospital investigations with regard to correct interpretation of VLAD including investigation of the relevant patient charts.
	11.1.5 Prepare the annual Public Hospital Performance Report.
	11.1.6 Assist with data analysis
	11.1.7 Assist with change management strategies
	11.1.8 Assist with implementation of improvements in care practices
	11.1.9 Review that there is evidence to support that the investigation has consulted each level of the Pyramid Model of Investigation.
11.2 **VLAD Review Subcommittee**	11.2.1 Assess whether the information reported that outlines an appropriate level of investigation has occurred
	11.2.2 Assess whether information reported outlines the formulation of an appropriate management action plan
	11.2.3 Ensure that the wording used to describe the above items is expressed in lay terms forthe purpose of collation and reporting within the annual Queensland Public Hospital

Figure A-2: The VLAD Implementation Standard, page 5 of 8

Clinical Governance, Variable Life Adjusted Display Dissemination and Reporting

Title /Role	Responsibilities
	Performance Report
11.3 **Patient Safety and Quality Board**	11.3.1 Provide advice to the Director-General on issues relating to patient safety, quality and effectiveness 11.3.2 Review level 3 flagged indicators and Level 3 VLAD Review Subcommittee recommendations
Area Level	
11.4 **General Managers, Area Health Services** **Chief Health Officer (for Private Facilities)**	11.4.1 Ensure flagged indicators are investigated and actioned by hospitals 11.4.2 Advise Patient Safety and Quality Board on lower level 3 flagged indicators and review outcomes 11.4.2 Ensure Districts submit reports within stipulated timeframes
11.5 **Clinical Networks and Collaboratives**	11.5.1 Assist with reviews of flagged indicators and outcomes 11.5.2 Assist with implementing management action plans where relevant
11.6 **Clinical Governance Unit** **Private Health Unit**	11.6.1 Advise General Managers Area Health Service/Chief Health Officer on reviews of flagged indicators and outcomes 11.6.2 Advise/engage with Clinical Networks/Collaboratives on reviews of flagged indicators and outcomes 11.6.3 Assist districts / private facilities with reviews of flagged indicators 11.6.4 Review District investigations to ensure management action plans address identified issues in the view of the Clinical Governance/Private Health Unit Manager
District/Facility Level	

Figure A-2: The VLAD Implementation Standard, page 6 of 8

Clinical Governance, Variable Life Adjusted Display Dissemination and Reporting

Title /Role	Responsibilities
11.7 **District Manager** **Clinical Chief Executive Officer** **Chief Executive Officer (Private Facility)**	11.7.1 Review hospital investigation and management action plan before submission 11.7.2 Ensure any changes identified have been actioned. 11.7.3 Nominate Lead Clinicians/Reviewers and other Appropriate Officers to view VLADs/assist reviews 11.7.4 Notify CPIC of Lead Clinicians/Reviewers and other Appropriate Officers
11.8 **Lead Clinician/ Reviewer**	11.8.1 Actively participate in hospital investigation of all flags 11.8.3 Notify District Manager/Clinical CEO of investigation outcome
11.9 **District Safety and Quality Committee**	11.9.1 Monitor reviews of flagged indicators and outcomes 11.9.2 Advise District Manager/Clinical CEO on review of all flagged indicators 11.9.3 Update District Clinical Risk Management Plan as a result of review of flagged indicators 11.9.4 Assess that the information reported outlines an appropriate level of investigation has occurred 11.9.5 Assess that information reported outlines the formulation of an appropriate management action plan
11.10 **Health Community Council**	11.10.1 Advise District Manager/Clinical CEO on issues relating to flagged indicators 11.10.2 Consider all VLADs and be satisfied that flagging VLADs have had appropriate action by the District Manager

12. Review Model

The VLAD is a quality monitoring tool and must be interpreted as such; it is designed to flag issues for further review. The occurrence of a flag should not be immediately interpreted as indicating good or bad performance as there are many possible explanations as to why the VLAD will flag, one reason being simply chance. Where review is initiated, it has been recommended that the pyramid model of investigation[1] be adopted (see Figure 1). In summary, the pyramid model of investigation suggests a hierarchical approach to identify causation. Under this model, factors at the base of the pyramid are more likely to be causes than factors at the apex.

---

[1] Mohammed MA, Rathbone A, Myers P, Patel D, Onions H, Stevens A. An investigation into general practitioners associated with high patient mortality flagged up through the Shipman inquiry: retrospective analysis of routine data. BMJ 2004; 328: 1474-7.

Figure A-2: The VLAD Implementation Standard, page 7 of 8

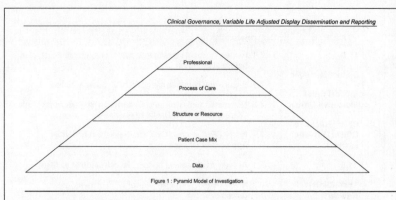

Clinical Governance, Variable Life Adjusted Display Dissemination and Reporting

Figure 1 : Pyramid Model of Investigation

13. Public Reporting

VLADs for each Hospital will be made available as part of the release of the Annual Public Hospital Performance Report required under the *Health Services Act 1991*. The Report should include the management action plans arising from the results of any hospital reviews conducted.

Release Details

Table A shows the administrative details for the current release of this document:

TABLE A	
Review authored by:	Kirstine Sketcher Baker/Kew Walker
	Date: April 2008
Approved by:	Patient Safety and Quality Board,
	Chair:
	Associate Professor Maarten Kamp
	_____
	(Approving Officer's Signature)

Figure A-2: The VLAD Implementation Standard, page 8 of 8

How Control Limits Are Worked Out

To identify variations that are not just due to the play of chance and where further investigation is likely to be useful, likelihood methods are used to inform setting upper and lower control limits. This process of assessing the play of chance is common to all areas of science and is termed statistical inference.

There are three main schools of statistical inference (that is, frameworks for assessing the play of chance): frequentist, Bayesian, and likelihood, although there is overlap in that likelihood calculations are used in both frequentist and Bayesian inference, and frequentist inference can be thought of as a particular type of Bayesian inference with a completely non-informative prior.

In any case, frequentist statistical inference (p-values and confidence intervals) remains the dominant method of statistical inference in medicine. But it is not well suited to control charts because the data for a particular hospital are looked at multiple times (that is, each time a patient is discharged). This means that p-values are difficult to interpret. More specifically, the Type 1 error rate is not constant, but increases with the length of the monitoring period. The probability of eventually signalling an alarm is 1.0 for all sequential tests, so that the Type 1 error rate will eventually be 100 per cent and the Type 2 error rate will eventually be 0 per cent.

Because p-values are problematic for control charts, the VLAD uses likelihood methods that have been used for control charts in industry since the 1950s. The statistical characteristics of the charts are defined in terms of the average run length to true or false alarm. Ideally, average run length to false alarm should be long (analogous to a low Type 1 error rate) and the average run length to true alarm should be short (analogous to high statistical power or a low Type 2 error rate). In practice, there is a trade-off. A good choice for a control limit, where the chart is said to signal, is one where the average run length to true alarm is suitably short and the average run length to false alarm is not unacceptably short.

Average run lengths (ARLs) for different control limits can be estimated using simulations, Markov chain analysis, or in certain circumstances by approximating formulae. For the VLADs we used simulations. Briefly, we specified data sets of 10 000 patients (under the null and various alternative hypotheses) and iterated 10 000 times to obtain estimates of the median ARL to true and false alarm.

The control limits are reset each time a trigger point is reached: a hospital that has previously hit a 50 per cent deviation from the average will be flagged, then the control limits are reset. The hospital will be flagged a second time if there is a cumulative run of cases which is again a 50 per cent deviation from the average, starting at the first trigger point.

Figure A-3: Understanding control limits, page 1 of 2.

The control limits indicate when chance has become an unlikely explanation for a hospital's deviation from the state average. At this point it becomes useful to look for causes other than chance, as per the Pyramid Model of investigation. As with any method of statistical inference, we cannot completely rule out chance as an explanation, but when control limits are reached chance is an unlikely explanation.

For more information on the technical background, see

Coory M, Sketcher-Baker K, Duckett S. Using control charts to monitor quality of hospital care with administrative data. *Int J Qual Health Care*, 2008 20: 31–9.

Grigg O, Farewell V, et al. Use of risk-adjusted CUSUM and RSPRT charts for monitoring in medical contexts. *Stat Meth Med Res* 2003 12: 147–70.

Sherlaw-Johnson C. A method for detecting runs of good and bad clinical outcomes on variable life-adjusted display (VLAD) charts. *Health Care Management Sc* 2005 8: 61–5.

Steiner S, Cook R, et al. Monitoring surgical performance using risk-adjusted cumulative sum charts. *Biostatistics* 2000 1: 441–52.

Figure A-3: Understanding control limits, page 2 of 2.

Appendix B

VLAD Clinical Indicator Definitions

● ●

*T*his appendix is divided into two sections. The tables in the first section list clinical indicator definitions and codes to use. The second section lists codes used for co-mortality risk assessment. For further information, email vlad_queries@health.qld.gov.au.

Outcome Indicator Definitions

Each table in this section provides a definition of the 30 outcome indicators currently used in VLADs.

Table B-1	Abdominal Hysterectomy Complications of Surgery
Definition	Defined as the number of records where any of the external cause codes was between Y60-Y6999 or Y83-Y8499, divided by the total number of records.
Inclusion and Exclusion Criteria	
Principal diagnosis codes and procedure codes	Any principal diagnosis code with at least one of the following procedure codes: 35653-00, 35653-01, 35653-02, 35653-03, 35661-00, 35667-00.
Separation date	From 1 July 2003 through till most recently extracted data from Data Services.
Episode type	Acute patients (epis_type = 01).
Overnight stay patients	Patients must have spent at least one night in hospital (end_date > start_date).
Age	20–89 years (age_grp >= 05 and age_grp <= 18).
Length of stay	1–30 patient days (pat_day >= 1 and pat_day <= 30).
Admission source	Excludes transfers in (orig-ref-code 24).
Separation mode	Excludes transfers out (sepn_mode 16).
Medical conditions	Exclude any condition code (principal diagnosis or other diagnosis) of malignant neoplasm of female genital organs or pelvic area (C18-C21, C48, C51-C58, C64-C68, C76.3, C77.5, C78.6, C79.6, C79.82).
Procedures	Exclude hysterectomies involving radical excision of pelvic lymph nodes (35664-00, 35670-00).
Major diagnostic category	Exclude MDC 14 (pregnancy, childbirth and puerperium) and exclude MDC 15 (newborns and other neonates).
Risk Adjustment Criteria	
Selected co-morbidities	Anaemia, hypertension, peritoneal adhesions, diseases of the circulatory system, intestinal disorders, urinary tract infection, other urinary symptoms.
	Indigenous status has not been used to adjust risk in this model, in order to focus hospital attention on improving outcomes for this group of patients.

Table B-2	AMI Long Stay
Definition	Long stay point = 14 days.
	For the purposes of this project, the long stay point was chosen as the day closest to the 90th percentile of all eligible length of stays. Therefore a long stay is defined as a record where the number of patient days equalled or exceeded the long stay point. Cases of in-hospital mortality prior to the long stay point were excluded from the calculation, but patients who died on or after the long stay point were included for this indicator.

Inclusion and Exclusion Criteria

Principal diagnosis codes	I21, I22.
State of usual residence	Queensland resident (state_id = 3).
Separation date	From 1 July 2003 through till most recently extracted data from Data Services.
Episode type	Acute patients (epis_type = 01).
Age	30–89 years (age_grp >= 07 and age_grp <= 18).
Additional criteria	The following procedure codes (invasive coronary procedures) were excluded from the analysis: 35304-00, 35304-01, 35305-00, 35305-01, 35310-00, 35310-01, 35310-02, 35310-03, 35310-04, 35310-05, 35335-00, 35338-00, 35338-01, 35341-00, 35344-00, 35344-01, 38215-00, 38218-00, 38218-01, 38218-02, 38497-00, 38497-01, 38497-02, 38497-03, 38497-04, 38497-05, 38497-06, 38497-07, 38500-00, 38500-01, 38500-02, 38500-03, 38500-04, 38503-00, 38503-01, 38503-02, 38503-03, 38503-04, 90201-00, 90201-01, 90201-02, 90201-03.
Length of stay	4–30 patient days (pat_day >= 4 and pat_day <= 30), unless the patient had a length of stay from 1 – 3 patient days and died in hospital (pat_day >= 1 and pat_day <= 3 and sepn_mode = 05).
Admission source	Admissions through the emergency department only (orig_ref_code = 02).
Separation mode	Exclude transfers out (sepn_mode ↑ 16).

Risk Adjustment Criteria

Selected co-morbidities	Anaemia, cellulitis, dysrhythmias, heart failure, hypotension, acute LRTI and influenza, renal disease.

Table B-3	AMI In-hospital Mortality
Definition	Defined as the records where separation mode = 05 (death) and length of stay was less than or equal to 30 days (pat_day <= 30). Same day deaths are included.

Inclusion and Exclusion Criteria

Principal diagnosis codes	I21, I22.
Separation date	From 1 July 2003 through till most recently extracted data from Data Services.
Episode type	Acute patients (epis_type = 01).
Age	30–89 years (age_grp >= 07 and age_grp <= 18).
Length of stay	4–30 patient days (pat_day >= 4 and pat_day <= 30), unless the patient had a length of stay from 1 – 3 patient days and died in hospital (pat_day >= 1 and pat_day <= 3 and sepn_mode = 05).
Admission source	Admissions through the emergency department only (orig_ref_code = 02).
Separation mode	Exclude transfers out (sepn_mode ↑ 16).

Risk Adjustment Criteria

Selected co-morbidities	Sex, age, malignancy, diabetes, dementia (including Alzheimer's disease), hypertension , dysrhythmias, heart failure, hypotension and shock, cerebrovascular disease, renal failure.
	Even though AMI morality odds ratio analysis for Aboriginal and Torres Strait Islanders is 1.6 (at 2005), Indigenous status has not been used to adjust risk in this model, in order to focus hospital attention on improving outcomes for this group of patients.

Table B-4	AMI Readmission
Definition	Patients readmitted to any Queensland hospital within 30 days of discharge for a condition that could be considered a consequence of the procedure (Diagnosis code: I21 and I22 and emergency admissions (elect_status = 1)). Readmissions were identified using probabilistic matching of identified data to allow inclusion of readmissions to a different facility as well as readmissions to the same facility. Episodes were matched using patient name (first name, surname and phonetic version of surname), date of birth, address (street, suburb and postcode), age and sex. To be considered a match, patients were required to be of the same sex and to have at least four of the other eight variables matching. A manual check was also conducted of potential matches to eliminate any false matches. Records were matched for acute episodes only to avoid counting hospitalisation for rehabilitation as a readmission.

Inclusion and Exclusion Criteria

Principal diagnosis codes	I21, I22.
State of usual residence	Queensland resident (state_id = 3).
Separation date	From 1 July 2003 through till most recently extracted data from Data Services.
Episode type	Acute patients (epis_type = 01).
Age	30–89 years (age_grp >= 07 and age_grp <= 18).
Additional criteria	Exclude transfers out (sepn_mode ↑ 16).
Admission source	Admissions through the emergency department only (orig_ref_code = 02).
Length of stay	4–30 patient days (pat_day >= 4 and pat_day <= 30).
Separation mode	Exclude in hospital deaths (sepn_mode ↑ 05).

Risk Adjustment Criteria

Selected co-morbidities	None.

Table B-5	Selected Primiparea Caesarean Section, Private Hospitals
Definition	Defined as records where method of delivery was lower section Caesarean section or classical Caesarean section (deliv_code = 4 or 5 or 04 or 05).

Inclusion and Exclusion Criteria

Separation date	From 1 July 2003 through till most recently extracted data from Data Services.
Mother's age group	20–34 years (moth_age_at_brth >= 20 and moth_age_at_brth <= 34).
Previous deliveries	No previous deliveries (pre_baby_alive<1 and pre_baby_not_alive <1).
Plurality	Singleton birth (plur = 1).
Period of gestation	37–41 completed weeks (gest_weeks >= 37 and gest_weeks <= 41).
Presentation	Vertex presentation (pres = 1).

Risk Adjustment Criteria

Selected co-morbidities	Sexually transmitted diseases, pre-existing hypertension complicating pregnancy with superimposed proteinuria, gestational diabetes, gestational hypertension/pre-eclampsia, prolonged rupture of membranes, baby weight group, placenta praevia with haemorrhage.
	Indigenous status has not been used to adjust risk in this model, in order to focus hospital attention on improving outcomes for this group of patients.

Table B-6	Selected Primiparea Caesarean Section, Public Hospitals
Definition	Defined as records where method of delivery was lower section Caesarean section or classical Caesarean section (deliv_code = 4 or 5 or 04 or 05).

Inclusion and Exclusion Criteria

Separation date	From 1 July 2003 through till most recently extracted data from Data Services.
Mother's age group	20–34 years (moth_age_at_brth >= 20 and moth_age_at_brth <= 34).
Previous deliveries	No previous deliveries (pre_baby_alive<1 and pre_baby_not_alive <1).
Plurality	Singleton birth (plur = 1).
Period of gestation	37–41 completed weeks (gest_weeks >= 37 and gest_weeks <= 41).
Presentation	Vertex presentation (pres = 1).

Risk Adjustment Criteria

Selected co-morbidities	Sexually transmitted diseases, pre-existing hypertension complicating pregnancy with superimposed proteinuria, gestational diabetes, gestational hypertension/pre-eclampsia, prolonged rupture of membranes, baby weight group, placenta praevia with haemorrhage. Indigenous status has not been used to adjust risk in this model, in order to focus hospital attention on improving outcomes for this group of patients.

Table B-7 Colorectal Carcinoma Complications of Surgery

Definition	Defined as the number of records where any of the external cause codes was between Y60-Y6999 or Y83-Y8499 for any episode of care within the entire hospital stay.

Inclusion and Exclusion Criteria

Principal diagnosis codes and procedure codes	Principal diagnosis code of C18-C20 or C21.8 with at least one of the following procedure codes: 32000-00, 32000-01, 32003-00, 32003-01, 32004-00, 32005-00, 32006-00, 32006-01, 32012-00, 32015-00, 32024-00, 32025-00, 32026-00, 32028-00, 32030-00, 32033-00, 32039-00, 32051-00, 32051-01.
Separation date	From 1 July 2003 through till most recently extracted data from Data Services.
Episode type	Acute patients (epis_type = 01).
Overnight stay patients	Patients must have spent at least one night in hospital (end_date > start_date).
Age	20 years or older (age_grp >= 05).
Length of stay	At least 4 patient days (pat_day >= 4), unless the patient had a length of stay from 1 – 3 patient days and died in hospital (pat_day >= 1 and pat_day <= 3 and sepn_mode = 05).
Admission source	Excludes transfers in (orig-ref-code ↑ 24).
Separation mode	Excludes transfers out (sepn_mode ↑ 16).

Risk Adjustment Criteria

Selected co-morbidities	Age, septicaemia, anaemia, diseases of the circulatory system, dysrhythmias, acute LRTI and influenza, intestinal disorders, peritoneal adhesions, renal disease, other urinary symptoms.

Indigenous status has not been used to adjust risk in this model, in order to focus hospital attention on improving outcomes for this group of patients. |

Table B-8	Depression Long Stay
Definition	Long stay point = 35 days. For the purposes of this project, the long stay point was chosen as 35 days as acute care certificates are 35 days.

Inclusion and Exclusion Criteria

Diagnosis-related group codes	DRGs of U63B and U64Z.
Separation date	From 1 July 2003 through till most recently extracted data from Data Services.
State of usual residence	Queensland resident (state_id = 3).
Episode type	Includes only patients admitted to acute psych units (stnd_unit_code = PYAA).
Age	18 to 64 years old.
Length of stay	Patients must have spent at least one night in hospital (end_date ^= start_date). Patients admitted for one night with a principal procedure code of 93340-02 or 93340-03 (electroconvulsive therapy) were also excluded.
Separation mode	Include home/usual residence, correctional facility and residential aged care service (sepn_mode = 01, 12 & 15).

Risk Adjustment Criteria

Selected co-morbidities	Age, circulatory diseases, intestinal disorders, social issues. Indigenous status has not been used to adjust risk in this model, in order to focus hospital attention on improving outcomes for this group of patients.

Table B-9	Depression Readmission
Definition	Patients readmitted to any Queensland hospital within 28 days of discharge with a DRG of Depression, admitted to acute psych units, Queensland residents and have stayed at least one night (two nights for patients admitted who had Electroconvulsive therapy). Readmissions were identified using probabilistic matching of identified data to allow inclusion of readmissions to a different facility as well as readmissions to the same facility. Episodes were matched using patient name (first name, surname and phonetic version of surname), date of birth, address (street, suburb and postcode), age and sex. To be considered a match, patients were required to be of the same sex and to have at least four of the other eight variables matching. A manual check was also conducted of potential matches to eliminate any false matches. Transfers out and in will not be included as readmissions as the separation of the initial period of care does not include transfers out.

Inclusion and Exclusion Criteria

Diagnosis-related group codes	DRGs of U63B and U64Z.
Separation date	From 1 July 2003 through till most recently extracted data from Data Services.
State of usual residence	Queensland resident (state_id = 3).
Episode type	Includes only patients admitted to acute psych units (stnd_unit_code = PYAA).
Age	18 to 64 years old.
Length of stay	Patients must have spent at least one night in hospital (end_date ^= start_date). Patients admitted for one night with a principal procedure code of 93340-02 or 93340-03 (Electroconvulsive therapy) were also excluded.
Separation mode	Include home/usual residence, correctional facility and residential aged care service (sepn_mode = 01, 12 & 15).

Risk Adjustment Criteria

Selected co-morbidities	Social issues. Indigenous status has not been used to adjust risk in this model, in order to focus hospital attention on improving outcomes for this group of patients.

Table B-10	Heart Failure Long Stay
Definition	Long stay point = 14 days. For the purposes of this project, the long stay point was chosen as the day closest to the 90th percentile of all eligible length of stays. Therefore a long stay is defined as a record where the number of patient days equalled or exceeded the long stay point. Cases of in-hospital mortality prior to the long stay point were excluded from the calculation, but patients who died on or after the long stay point were included for this indicator.

Inclusion and Exclusion Criteria

Principal diagnosis code	I50.
Separation date	From 1 July 2003 through till most recently extracted data from Data Services.
State of usual residence	Queensland resident (state_id = 3).
Episode type	Acute patients (epis_type = 01).
Overnight stay patients	Patients must have spent at least one night in hospital (end_date > start_date).
Age	30–89 years (age_grp >= 07 and age_grp <= 18).
Length of stay	1–30 patient days (pat_day >= 1 and pat_day <= 30).
Admission source	Excludes transfers in (orig-ref-code ↑ 24).
Separation mode	Excludes transfers out (sepn_mode ↑ 16).

Risk Adjustment Criteria

Selected co-morbidities	Age, septicaemia, malignancy, anaemia, hyponatremia, valvular disorders, dysrhythmias, cerebrovascular disease, hypotension and shock, acute LRTI and influenza, other chronic obstructive pulmonary disease, intestinal disorders, liver disease, cellulitis, ulcer of lower limb or decubitus ulcer, renal failure, urinary tract infection (site not specified), other urinary symptoms, oedema. Indigenous status has not been used to adjust risk in this model, in order to focus hospital attention on improving outcomes for this group of patients.

Table B-11	Heart Failure In-hospital Mortality
Definition	Defined as the number of records where separation mode = 05 (death) and length of stay was less than or equal to 30 days (pat_day <= 30).

Inclusion and Exclusion Criteria

Principal diagnosis code	I50.
Separation date	From 1 July 2003 through till most recently extracted data from Data Services.
Episode type	Acute patients (epis_type = 01).
Overnight stay patients	Patients must have spent at least one night in hospital (end_date > start_date).
Age	30–89 years (age_grp > = 07 and age_grp <= 18).
Length of stay	1–30 patient days (pat_day > = 1 and pat_day <= 30).
Admission source	Excludes transfers in (orig-ref-code ↑ 24).
Separation mode	Excludes transfers out (sepn_mode ↑ 16).

Risk Adjustment Criteria

Selected co-morbidities	Age, septicaemia, malignancy, dementia (including Alzheimer's disease), hypertension, ischaemic heart disease, dysrhythmias, acute LRTI and influenza, ulcer of lower limb or decubitus ulcer, renal failure, hypotension and shock, cerebrovascular disease.
	Indigenous status has not been used to adjust risk in this model, in order to focus hospital attention on improving outcomes for this group of patients.

Table B-12	Heart Failure Readmission
Definition	Patients readmitted to any Queensland hospital within 30 days of discharge for a condition that could be considered a consequence of the procedure (Diagnosis code: I50). Readmissions were identified using probabilistic matching of identified data to allow inclusion of readmissions to a different facility as well as readmissions to the same facility. Episodes were matched using patient name (first name, surname and phonetic version of surname), date of birth, address (street, suburb and postcode), age and sex. To be considered a match, patients were required to be of the same sex and to have at least four of the other eight variables matching. A manual check was also conducted of potential matches to eliminate any false matches. Records were matched for acute episodes only to avoid counting hospitalisation for rehabilitation as a readmission.

Inclusion and Exclusion Criteria

Principal diagnosis code	I50.
Separation date	From 1 July 2003 through till most recently extracted data from Data Services.
State of usual residence	Queensland resident (state_id = 3).
Episode type	Acute patients (epis_type = 01).
Overnight stay patients	Patients must have spent at least one night in hospital (end_date > start_date).
Age	30–89 years (age_grp >= 07 and age_grp <= 18).
Length of stay	1–30 patient days (pat_day >= 1 and pat_day <= 30).
Admission source	Excludes transfers in (orig-ref-code ↑ 24).
Separation mode	Excludes transfers out (sepn_mode ↑ 16).
Separation mode	Excludes deaths (sepn_mode ↑ 05).

Risk Adjustment Criteria

Selected co-morbidities	Age, sex.
	Indigenous status has not been used to adjust risk in this model, in order to focus hospital attention on improving outcomes for this group of patients.

Table B-13   Hip Replacement Complications of Surgery

Definition	Defined as the number of records where any of the external cause codes was between Y60-Y6999 or Y83-Y8499.

Inclusion and Exclusion Criteria

Principal diagnosis codes and procedure codes	Any principal diagnosis code with at least one of the following procedure codes: 49318-00, 49319-00.
Separation date	From 1 July 2003 through till most recently extracted data from Data Services.
Episode type	Acute patients (epis_type = 01).
Age	20 years or older (age_grp >= 05).
Length of stay	3 patient days or longer (pat_day >= 3).
Admission source	Excludes transfers in (orig-ref-code 24).
Separation mode	Exclude transfers out (sepn_mode 16). In the case of changes of episode (sepn_mode 06), immediately ensuing non-acute episodes (e.g. rehabilitation) were appended to the original acute episode to form a complete record of the hospital stay, including non-acute episodes that extended into the next analysis period.

Risk Adjustment Criteria

Selected co-morbidities	Age, anaemia, diseases of the circulatory system, renal disease, other urinary symptoms.
	Indigenous status has not been used to adjust risk in this model, in order to focus hospital attention on improving outcomes for this group of patients.

Table B-14	Hip Replacement Long Stay
Definition	Long stay point = 14 days. For the purposes of this project, the long stay point was chosen as the day closest to the 90th percentile of all eligible length of stays. Therefore a long stay is defined as a record where the number of patient days equalled or exceeded the long stay point. Cases of in-hospital mortality prior to the long stay point were excluded from the calculation, but patients who died on or after the long stay point were included for this indicator.

Inclusion and Exclusion Criteria

Principal diagnosis codes and procedure codes	Any principal diagnosis code with at least one of the following procedure codes: 49318-00, 49319-00.
Separation date	From 1 July 2003 through till most recently extracted data from Data Services.
State of usual residence	Queensland resident (state_id = 3).
Length of stay	3 patient days or longer (pat_day >= 3).
Episode type	Acute patients (epis_type = 01).
Age	20 years or older (age_grp >= 05).
Admission source	Excludes transfers in (orig-ref-code 24).
Separation mode	Exclude transfers out (sepn_mode 16). In the case of changes of episode (sepn_mode 06), immediately ensuing non-acute episodes (e.g. rehabilitation) were appended to the original acute episode to form a complete record of the hospital stay, including non-acute episodes that extended into the next analysis period.

Risk Adjustment Criteria

Selected co-morbidities	Age, anaemia, ischaemic heart disease, dysrhythmia, ulcer of lower limb or decubitus ulcer, renal disease.

Indigenous status has not been used to adjust risk in this model, in order to focus hospital attention on improving outcomes for this group of patients. |

Table B-15	Hip Replacement Readmission
Definition	Patients readmitted to any Queensland hospital within 60 days of discharge to home / usual residence (sepn_mode = 01) for a condition that could be considered a consequence of the procedure. Relevant ICD codes are: G46, I21, I26, I50, I621, I633, I74, I80, I978, J15, J180, J189, J958, L039, L0311, L89, M256, M968, N13, N30, N390, R33, S7200, S7208, S73, T811, T813, T815, T816, T818, T819, T84, T8578, T8588, T859, T887, T89. Readmissions were identified using probabilistic matching of identified data to allow inclusion of readmissions to a different facility as well as readmissions to the same facility. Episodes were matched using patient name (first name, surname and phonetic version of surname), date of birth, address (street, suburb and postcode), age and sex. To be considered a match, patients were required to be of the same sex and to have at least four of the other eight variables matching. A manual check was also conducted of potential matches to eliminate any false matches. Records were matched for acute episodes only to avoid counting transfers as a readmission.

Inclusion and Exclusion Criteria

Principal diagnosis codes and procedure codes	Any principal diagnosis code with at least one of the following procedure codes: 49318-00, 49319-00.
Separation date	Between 1 July 2003 through till most recently extracted data from Data Services.
State of usual residence	Queensland resident (state_id = 3).
Episode type	Acute patients (epis_type = 01).
Age	20 years or older (age_grp >= 05).
Length of stay	3 patient days or longer (pat_day >= 3).
Admission source	Excludes transfers in (orig-ref-code 24).
Separation mode	Exclude transfers out (sepn_mode 16). In the case of changes of episode (sepn_mode 06), immediately ensuing non-acute episodes (e.g. rehabilitation) were appended to the original acute episode to form a complete record of the hospital stay, including non-acute episodes that extended into the next analysis period.

Risk Adjustment Criteria

Co-morbidities	None.

Table B-16	Induced Births (Selected Primiparea)
Definition	Defined as records where the onset of labour was induced (labour_onset = 2).

Inclusion and Exclusion Criteria

Separation date	From 1 July 2003 through till most recently extracted data from Data Services.
Mother's age group	20–34 years (moth_age_at_brth >= 20 and moth_age_at_brth <= 34).
Previous deliveries	No previous deliveries (pre_baby_alive<1 and pre_baby_not_alive <1).
Plurality	Singleton birth (plur = 1).
Period of gestation	37–41 completed weeks (gest_weeks >= 37 and gest_weeks <= 41).
Presentation	Vertex presentation (pres = 1).

Risk Adjustment Criteria

Selected co-morbidities	Baby weight group, gestational diabetes, pre-existing hypertension complicating pregnancy with superimposed proteinuria, gestational hypertension/pre-eclampsia, prolonged rupture of membranes. Indigenous status has not been used to adjust risk in this model, in order to focus hospital attention on improving outcomes for this group of patients.

Table B-17	Knee Replacement Primary Complications of Surgery
Definition	Defined as the number of records where any of the external cause codes was between Y60-Y6999 or Y83-Y8499.

Inclusion and Exclusion Criteria

Principal diagnosis codes and procedure codes	Any principal diagnosis code with at least one of the following procedure codes: 49518-00, 49519-00, 49521-02.
Separation date	From 1 July 2003 through till most recently extracted data from Data Services.
Episode type	Acute patients (epis_type = 01).
Age	20 years or older (age_grp >= 05).
Length of stay	4 patient days or longer (pat_day >= 4).
Admission source	Excludes transfers in (orig-ref-code 24).
Separation mode	Exclude transfers out (sepn_mode 16). In the case of changes of episode (sepn_mode 06), immediately ensuing non-acute episodes (e.g. rehabilitation) were appended to the original acute episode to form a complete record of the hospital stay, including non-acute episodes that extended into the next analysis period.

Risk Adjustment Criteria

Selected co-morbidities	Anaemia, diseases of the circulatory system, dysrhythmias, acute LRTI and influenza, intestinal disorders, renal disease, other urinary symptoms.
	Indigenous status has not been used to adjust risk in this model, in order to focus hospital attention on improving outcomes for this group of patients.

Table B-18	Knee Replacement (Primary) Long Stay
Definition	Long stay point = 12 days.
	For the purposes of this project, the long stay point was chosen as the day closest to the 90th percentile of all eligible length of stays. Therefore a long stay is defined as a record where the number of patient days equalled or exceeded the long stay point. Cases of in-hospital mortality prior to the long stay point were excluded from the calculation, but patients who died on or after the long stay point were included for this indicator.

Inclusion and Exclusion Criteria

Principal diagnosis codes and procedure codes	Any principal diagnosis code with at least one of the following procedure codes: 49518-00, 49519-00, 49521-02.
Separation date	From 1 July 2003 through till most recently extracted data from Data Services.
State of usual residence	Queensland resident (state_id = 3).
Episode type	Acute patients (epis_type = 01).
Age	20 years or older (age_grp >= 05).
Length of stay	4 patient days or longer (pat_day >= 4).
Admission source	Excludes transfers in (orig-ref-code 24).
Separation mode	Exclude transfers out (sepn_mode 16). In the case of changes of episode (sepn_mode 06), immediately ensuing non-acute episodes (e.g. rehabilitation) were appended to the original acute episode to form a complete record of the hospital stay, including non-acute episodes that extended into the next analysis period.

Risk Adjustment Criteria

Selected co-morbidities	Age, diseases of the circulatory system, hypertension, intestinal disorders, ulcer of lower limb or decubitus ulcer, renal disease, other urinary symptoms.
	Indigenous status has not been used to adjust risk in this model, in order to focus hospital attention on improving outcomes for this group of patients.

Table B-19	Knee Replacement (Primary) Readmission
Definition	Patients readmitted to any Queensland hospital within 60 days of discharge to home / usual residence (sepn_ mode = 01) for a condition that could be considered a consequence of the procedure. Relevant ICD codes are : I21, I26, I50, I74, I801, I802, I978, J151, J180, J189, J958, L0311, L892, M17, M23, M246, M256, N13, N390, R33, S7210, S820, S8344, S89, T81, T84, T8578, T8588, T887. Readmissions were identified using probabilistic matching of identified data to allow inclusion of readmissions to a different facility as well as readmissions to the same facility. Episodes were matched using patient name (first name, surname and phonetic version of surname), date of birth, address (street, suburb and postcode), age and sex. To be considered a match, patients were required to be of the same sex and to have at least four of the other eight variables matching. A manual check was also conducted of potential matches to eliminate any false matches. Records were matched for acute episodes only to avoid counting hospitalisation for rehabilitation as a readmission. Transfers in and out were also excluded to avoid counting transfers as a readmission.

Inclusion and Exclusion Criteria

Principal diagnosis codes and procedure codes	Any principal diagnosis code with at least one of the following procedure codes: 49518-00, 49519-00, 49521-02.
Separation date	From 1 July 2003 through till most recently extracted data from Data Services.
State of usual residence	Queensland resident (state_id = 3).
Episode type	Acute patients (epis_type = 01).
Age	20 years or older (age_grp >= 05).
Length of stay	4 patient days or longer (pat_day >= 4).
Admission source	Excludes transfers in (orig-ref-code 24).
Separation mode	Exclude transfers out (sepn_mode 16). In the case of changes of episode (sepn_mode 06), immediately ensuing non-acute episodes (e.g. rehabilitation) were appended to the original acute episode to form a complete record of the hospital stay, including non-acute episodes that extended into the next analysis period.

Risk Adjustment Criteria

Selected co-morbidities	None.

Table B-20   Laparoscopic Cholecystectomy Complications of Surgery

Definition	Defined as the number of records where any of the external cause codes was between Y60-Y6999 or Y83-Y8499.

Inclusion and Exclusion Criteria

Principal diagnosis codes and procedure codes	Any diagnosis code with at least 30445-00 as a procedure code.
Separation date	From 1 July 2003 through till most recently extracted data from Data Services.
Episode type	Acute patients (epis_type = 01).
Age	20 years or older (age_grp >= 05).
Length of stay	0–30 patient days (pat_day >= 0 and pat_day <= 30).
Admission source	Excludes transfers in (orig-ref-code 24).
Separation mode	Excludes transfers out (sepn_mode 16).
Elective status	Planned elective patients only (elect_status = 2).

Risk Adjustment Criteria

Selected co-morbidities	Sex, age, malignancy, hypertension, ischaemic heart disease, dysrhythmias, peritoneal adhesions, liver disease. Indigenous status has not been used to adjust risk in this model, in order to focus hospital attention on improving outcomes for this group of patients.

Table B-21	Fractured Neck of Femur Complications of Surgery
Definition	Defined as the number of records where any of the external cause codes was between Y60-Y6999 or Y83-Y8499.

Inclusion and Exclusion Criteria

Principal diagnosis codes and procedure codes	Principal diagnosis code of S72 with at least one of the following procedure codes: 47519.00, 47522.00, 47528.01, 47531.00 or 49315.00.
Separation date	From 1 July 2003 through till most recently extracted data from Data Services.
Episode type	Acute patients (epis_type = 01).
Age	50 years or older (age_grp >= 11).
Overnight patients	Patients must have spent at least one night in hospital (end_date > start_date).
Admission source	Excludes transfers in (orig-ref-code 24).
Separation mode	Excludes transfers out (sepn_mode 16). In the case of changes of episode (sepn_mode = 06), immediately ensuing non-acute episodes (e.g. rehabilitation) were appended to the original acute episode to form a complete record of the hospital stay, including non-acute episodes that extended into the next analysis period.
External cause	Principal external cause of falls (ex_1 >= W00 and ex_1 <= W1999).

Risk Adjustment Criteria

Selected co-morbidities	Anaemia, diseases of the circulatory system, dysrhythmias, intestinal disorders, other urinary symptoms.
	Indigenous status has not been used to adjust risk in this model, in order to focus hospital attention on improving outcomes for this group of patients.

Table B-22   Fractured Neck of Femur In-hospital Mortality

Definition	Defined as the number of records where separation mode = 05 (death) and length of stay was less than or equal to 30 days (pat_day <= 30).

Inclusion and Exclusion Criteria

Principal diagnosis codes and procedure codes	Principal diagnosis code of S72 with at least one of the following procedure codes: 47519.00, 47522.00, 47528.01, 47531.00 or 49315.00.
Separation date	From 1 July 2003 through till most recently extracted data from Data Services.
Episode type	Acute patients (epis_type = 01).
Age	50 years or older (age_grp >= 11).
Overnight patients	Patients must have spent at least one night in hospital (end_date > start_date).
Admission source	Excludes transfers in (orig-ref-code 24).
Separation mode	Excludes transfers out (sepn_mode 16). In the case of changes of episode (sepn_mode = 06), immediately ensuing non-acute episodes (e.g. rehabilitation) were appended to the original acute episode to form a complete record of the hospital stay, including non-acute episodes that extended into the next analysis period.
External cause	Principal external cause of falls (ex_1 >= W00 and ex_1 <= W1999).

Risk Adjustment Criteria

Selected co-morbidities	Sex, age, ischaemic heart disease, dysrhythmias, heart failure, acute LRTI and influenza, renal failure.
	Indigenous status has not been used to adjust risk in this model, in order to focus hospital attention on improving outcomes for this group of patients.

Table B-23   Paediatric Tonsillectomy and Adenoidectomy
Long Stay

Definition	Long stay point = 2 days.
	For the purposes of this project, the long stay point was chosen as the day closest to the 90th percentile of all eligible length of stays. Therefore a long stay is defined as a record where the number of patient days equalled or exceeded the long stay point.

Inclusion and Exclusion Criteria

Procedure codes	Procedure code of 41789-00, 41801-00 or 41789-01.
State of usual residence	Queensland resident (state_id = 3).
Separation date	From 1 July 2003 through till most recently extracted data from Data Services.
Episode type	Acute patients (epis_type = 01).
Age	0–14 years (age_grp <= 03).
Admission source	Exclude transfers in (orig_ref_code ↑ 24). Include same day patients.
Separation mode	Exclude transfers out (sepn_mode ↑ 16) and excludes deaths (sepn_mode ↑ 05).

Risk Adjustment Criteria

Selected co-morbidities	Age.
	Indigenous status has not been used to adjust risk in this model, in order to focus hospital attention on improving outcomes for this group of patients.

Table B-24   Paediatric Tonsillectomy and Adenoidectomy Readmission

Definition	Patients readmitted to any Queensland hospital within 15 days of discharge to home/usual residence (sepn_mode = 01) for a condition that could be considered a consequence of the procedure. Relevant ICD codes are: E86, E898, E899, J03, J06, J18 - J22, J35 - J36, J958, J959, K910, K918, K919, K920, R040, R070, R11, R50, R53, R56, R58, T81, T888, T8899, Z038, Z039 and Z48. Readmissions were identified using probabilistic matching of identified data to allow inclusion of readmissions to a different facility as well as readmissions to the same facility. Episodes were matched using patient name (first name, surname and phonetic version of surname), date of birth, address (street, suburb and postcode), age and sex. To be considered a match, patients were required to be of the same sex and to have at least four of the other eight variables matching. A manual check was also conducted of potential matches to eliminate any false matches. Records were matched for acute episodes only to avoid counting hospitalisation for rehabilitation as a readmission.

Inclusion and Exclusion Criteria

Procedure codes	Procedure code of 41789-00, 41801-00 or 41789-01.
State of usual residence	Queensland resident (state_id = 3).
Separation date	From 1 July 2003 through till most recently extracted data from Data Services.
Episode type	Acute patients (epis_type = 01).
Age	0–14 years (age_grp <= 03).
Length of stay	0–30 patient days (pat_day >= 0 and pat_day <= 30).
Admission source	Exclude transfers in (orig_ref_code ↑ 24). Include same day patients.
Separation mode	Exclude transfers out (sepn_mode ↑ 16) and excludes deaths (sepn_mode ↑ 05).

Risk Adjustment Criteria

Selected co-morbidities	None. Indigenous status has not been used to adjust risk in this model, in order to focus hospital attention on improving outcomes for this group of patients.

Table B-25	Pneumonia In-hospital Mortality
Definition	Defined as the number of records where separation mode = 05 (death) and length of stay was less than or equal to 30 days (pat_day <= 30).

Inclusion and Exclusion Criteria

Principal diagnosis code	J13-J16, J18.
Separation date	From 1 July 2003 through till most recently extracted data from Data Services.
Episode type	Acute patients (epis_type = 01).
Overnight stay patients	Patients must have spent at least one night in hospital (end_date > start_date).
Age	20–89 years (age_grp >= 05 and age_grp <= 18).
Length of stay	1–30 patient days (pat_day >= 1 and pat_day <= 30).
Admission source	Excludes transfers in (orig-ref-code 24).
Separation mode	Excludes transfers out (sepn_mode 16).

Risk Adjustment Criteria

Selected co-morbidities	Age, septicaemia, malignancy, dementia (including Alzheimer's disease), Parkinson's disease, dysrhythmias, heart failure, hypotension and shock, cerebrovascular disease, other chronic obstructive pulmonary disease, liver disease, ulcer of lower limb or decubitus ulcer, renal failure.
	Indigenous status has not been used to adjust risk in this model, in order to focus hospital attention on improving outcomes for this group of patients.

Table B-26	Prostatectomy Complications of Surgery
Definition	Defined as the number of records where any of the external cause codes was between Y60-Y6999 or Y83-Y8499.

Inclusion and Exclusion Criteria

Principal diagnosis codes and procedure codes	Any diagnosis code with 37203-00 as a procedure code.
Separation date	From 1 July 2003 through till most recently extracted data from Data Services.
Episode type	Acute patients (epis_type = 01).
Length of stay	0–30 patient days (pat_day >= 0 and pat_day <= 30).
Age	20 years or older (age_grp >= 05).
Admission source	Excludes transfers in (orig-ref-code 24).
Separation mode	Excludes transfers out (sepn_mode 16).
Sex	Male (sex = 1).

Risk Adjustment Criteria

Selected co-morbidities	Anaemia, diseases of the circulatory system, dysrhythmias, urinary tract infection (site not specified), other urinary symptoms.
	Indigenous status has not been used to adjust risk in this model, in order to focus hospital attention on improving outcomes for this group of patients.

Table B-27	Schizophrenia Long Stay
Definition	Long stay point = 35 days.
	For the purposes of this project, the long stay point was chosen as 35 days as acute care certificates are 35 days.

Inclusion and Exclusion Criteria

Diagnosis-related group codes	DRG of U61A and U61B.
Separation date	From 1 July 2003 through till most recently extracted data from Data Services.
State of usual residence	Queensland resident (state_id = 3).
Episode type	Includes only patients admitted to acute psych units (stnd_unit_code = PYAA).
Age	18 to 64 years old.
Length of stay	Patients must have spent at least one night in hospital (end_date ^= start_date). Patients admitted for one night with a principal procedure code of 93340-02 or 93340-03 (Electroconvulsive therapy) were also excluded.
Separation mode	Include home/usual residence, correctional facility and residential aged care service (sepn_mode = 01, 12 & 15).

Risk Adjustment Criteria

Selected co-morbidities	Age, anaemia, circulatory diseases, hypotension, acute upper RTI, acute LRTI and influenza, intestinal disorders, cellulitis, dorsalgia, renal disease, other urinary symptoms.
	Indigenous status has not been used to adjust risk in this model, in order to focus hospital attention on improving outcomes for this group of patients.

Table B-28	Schizophrenia Readmission
Definition	Patients readmitted to any Queensland hospital within 28 days of discharge with a DRG of Schizophrenia, admitted to acute psych units, Queensland residents and have stayed at least one night (two nights for patients admitted who had Electroconvulsive therapy). Readmissions were identified using probabilistic matching of identified data to allow inclusion of readmissions to a different facility as well as readmissions to the same facility. Episodes were matched using patient name (first name, surname and phonetic version of surname), date of birth, address (street, suburb and postcode), age and sex. To be considered a match, patients were required to be of the same sex and to have at least four of the other eight variables matching. A manual check was also conducted of potential matches to eliminate any false matches. Transfers out and in will not be included as readmissions as the separation of the initial period of care does not include transfers out.

Inclusion and Exclusion Criteria

Diagnosis-related group codes	DRG of U61A and U61B.
Separation date	From 1 July 2003 through till most recently extracted data from Data Services.
State of usual residence	Queensland resident (state_id = 3).
Episode type	Includes only patients admitted to acute psych units (stnd_unit_code = PYAA).
Age	18 to 64 years old.
Length of stay	Patients must have spent at least one night in hospital (end_date ^= start_date). Patients admitted for one night with a principal procedure code of 93340-02 or 93340-03 (Electroconvulsive therapy) were also excluded.
Separation mode	Include home/usual residence, correctional facility and residential aged care service (sepn_mode = 01, 12 & 15).

Risk Adjustment Criteria

Selected co-morbidities	Age.
	Indigenous status has not been used to adjust risk in this model, in order to focus hospital attention on improving outcomes for this group of patients.

Table B-29	Stroke In-hospital Mortality
Definition	Defined as the number of records where separation mode = 05 (death) and length of stay was less than or equal to 30 days (pat_day <= 30).

Inclusion and Exclusion Criteria

Principal diagnosis code	I61–I64
Separation date	From 1 July 2003 through till most recently extracted data from Data Services.
Episode type	Acute patients (epis_type = 01).
Length of stay	3 or more patient days unless the patient died in hospital (pat_days >= 3 or sepn_mode = 05).
Age	30–89 years (age_grp >= 07 and age_grp <= 18).
Admission source	Excludes transfers in (orig-ref-code ↑ 24) and changes of episode type (orig_ref_code ↑ 06).
Separation mode	Exclude transfers out (sepn_mode ↑ 16). In the case of changes of episode (sepn_mode = 06), immediately ensuing non-acute episodes (e.g. rehabilitation) were appended to the original acute episode to form a complete record of the hospital stay, including non-acute episodes that extended into the next analysis period.
Procedures	Exclude carotid endarterectomy (33500-00 or 32703-00).

Risk Adjustment Criteria

Selected co-morbidities	Age, septicaemia, malignancy, heart failure, acute LRTI and influenza, renal failure.
	Indigenous status has not been used to adjust risk in this model, in order to focus hospital attention on improving outcomes for this group of patients.

Table B-30	Vaginal Hysterectomy Complications of Surgery
Definition	Defined as the number of records where any of the external cause codes was between Y60-Y6999 or Y83-Y8499, divided by the total number of records.

Inclusion and Exclusion Criteria

Principal diagnosis codes and procedure codes	Any principal diagnosis code with at least one of the following procedure codes: 35657-00, 35667-01, 35750-00, 35673-00, 35673-01, 35753-00, 35753-01.
Separation date	From 1 July 2003 through till most recently extracted data from Data Services.
Episode type	Acute patients (epis_type = 01).
Overnight stay patients	Patients must have spent at least one night in hospital (end_date > start_date).
Age	20–89 years (age_grp >= 05 and age_grp <= 18).
Length of stay	1–30 patient days (pat_day >= 1 and pat_day <= 30).
Admission source	Excludes transfers in (orig-ref-code ↑ 24).
Separation mode	Excludes transfers out (sepn_mode ↑ 16).
Medical conditions	Exclude any condition code (principal diagnosis or other diagnosis) of malignant neoplasm of female genital organs or pelvic area (C18-C21, C48, C51-C58, C64-C68, C76.3, C77.5, C78.6, C79.6, C79.82).
Procedures	Exclude hysterectomies involving radical excision of pelvic lymph nodes (35664-01).
Major diagnostic category	Exclude MDC 14 (pregnancy, childbirth and puerperium) and exclude MDC 15 (newborns and other neonates).

Risk Adjustment Criteria

Selected co-morbidities	Anaemia, diseases of the circulatory system, urinary tract infection, other urinary symptoms.
	Indigenous status has not been used to adjust risk in this model, in order to focus hospital attention on improving outcomes for this group of patients.

Co-morbidity Codes

The following table lists ICD-10.5-AM codes for co-morbidities, used for risk adjustment.

Table B-31	Risk-Adjustment Codes
Co-morbidity	*ICD-10.5-AM Code*
Septicaemia	A40–A41
Respiratory syndrome	B974–B974
Malignancy	C00–C97
Anaemia	D50–D64
Disorders of thyroid gland	E00–E07
Diabetes	E10–E14
Hyponatremia	E871
Dementia (including Alzheimer's disease)	F00–F03, G30–G311
Parkinson's disease	G20
Epilepsy	G40–G41
Migraine	G43
Polyneuropathy (unspecified)	G629
Hemiplegia	G81
Other retinal disorders	H35
Diseases of the circulatory system	I00–I99
Valvular disorders	I05–I08, I33–I39
Hypertension	I10–I15
Ischaemic heart disease	I20–I25
Cardiomyopathy	I42, I43
Conduction disorders	I44, I45
Dysrhythmias	I46–I49
Heart failure	I50
Cerebrovascular disease	I60–I69
Peripheral vascular disease	I70–I74

Co-morbidity	ICD-10.5-AM Code
Hypotension and shock	I95, R57
Acute upper RTI	J00–J0699
Acute LRTI and influenza	J9–J22
Upper respiratory disease	J399
Asthma	J45, J46
Other chronic obstructive pulmonary disease	J40–J44, J47
Intestinal disorders	K21, K52–K59
Peritoneal adhesions	K660
Liver disease	K70–K77
Cellulitis	L03
Ulcer of lower limb or decubitus ulcer	L89, L97
Dorsalgia	M54
Renal disease	N00–N39
Renal failure	N17–N19, R34
Urinary tract infection (site not specified)	N390, T835
Gangrene (not elsewhere classified)	R02
Other urinary symptoms	R30–R39
Oedema	R60
AMI-Specific Codes	
Diabetes without complications	E101, E105, E106, E109, E110, E111, E115, E116, E119, E130, E131, E135, E136, E139, E140, E141, E145, E146, E149
Rheumatologic disease	M05–M09, M30–M36
Mental Health-Specific Codes	
Open wound of wrist or hand	S61
Burns	T20–T31
Poisoning	T36–T50
Social issues	Z55–Z78

(continued)

Table B-31 *(continued)*

Maternity-Specific Codes

Sexually transmitted diseases	A50– A64
Herpes	A60
Viral infection – unspecified	B349–B34
Pre-existing hypertension complicating pregnancy	O10
Pre-existing hypertension complicating pregnancy with superimposed proteinuria	O11–O1199
Gestational hypertension without significant proteinuria	O13
Gestational hypertension/pre-eclampsia	O13–O1699
Gestational hypertension with significant proteinuria	O14
Haemorrhage in early pregnancy	O20
Gestational diabetes	O2441, O2442, O2449
Prolonged rupture of membranes	O4211, O4212 or O429
Placenta praevia with haemorrhage	O44–O46
Premature separation of placenta	O45
Antepartum haemorrhage, not elsewhere classified	O46
Gestational weeks	Collected in Perinatal Data Collection
Baby weight group	Collected in Perinatal Data Collection
Plurality	Collected in Perinatal Data Collection
Delivery code	Collected in Perinatal Data Collection
Congenital anomalies	Collected in Perinatal Data Collection

Index

Notes

. . . .

_____

_____

_____

_____

_____

_____

_____

_____

_____

_____

_____

_____

_____

_____

_____

_____

_____

_____

_____

_____

_____

_____

Notes

Notes

. . . .

_____

_____

_____

_____

_____

_____

_____

_____

_____

_____

_____

_____

_____

_____

_____

_____

_____

_____

_____

_____

Notes